UNFINISHED DESIGN

THE HUMANITIES AND SOCIAL SCIENCES IN UNDERGRADUATE ENGINEERING EDUCATION

JOSEPH S. JOHNSTON, JR.
Director of Programs
Association of American Colleges

SUSAN SHAMAN
Associate Director
Institute for Research on Higher Education
University of Pennsylvania

ROBERT ZEMSKY
Director
Institute for Research on Higher Education
University of Pennsylvania

ASSOCIATION OF AMERICAN COLLEGES, 1988

THIS WORK WAS SUPPORTED
BY THE ANDREW W. MELLON FOUNDATION
AND THE PEW MEMORIAL TRUST.

Cover: *Computer Composition With Lines*
Computer-generated art by A. Michael Noll, © 1965.
As reproduced in
Digital Visions: Computers and Art
by Cynthia Goodman
© 1987 Harry N. Abrams and Everson Museum.

Photograph opposite page 1:
University of Virginia
Bill Sublette

Published by
Association of American Colleges
1818 R Street, NW
Washington, D.C. 20009

Copyright 1988

ISBN 0-911696-42-3

CONTENTS

1
INTRODUCTION

5
CHAPTER ONE
UNFINISHED DESIGN

The Rationale for Liberal Education 7

Dimensions of the Problem 9

13
CHAPTER TWO
AN ANALYSIS: PROGRAM POLICY AND STUDENT PRACTICE

Engineering Program Policy on H&SS Coursework 14

Student Practice in Selecting Courses 24

33
CHAPTER THREE
INNOVATIVE PROGRAMS

63
CHAPTER FOUR
CRITERIA AND STRATEGIES

Essential Undergraduate Experiences 64

Key Criteria for Coursework 66

Administrative Strategies 68

Improving H&SS Academic Advising 69

Finding Principles of Coherence 70

Some Sample Course Clusters 74

Integrating Learning 76

79
REFERENCES

INTRODUCTION

In January 1986 the Association of American Colleges (AAC) undertook a major project with support from the Andrew W. Mellon Foundation. The purpose of this two-and-a-half year effort has been to improve the quality and coherence of the humanities and social sciences (H&SS) coursework of undergraduate engineering students. Generously assisted by individuals and organizations from the worlds both of engineering and of liberal arts education and by an additional grant from the Pew Memorial Trust, AAC has completed the initial phases of the project: a study of engineering programs' H&SS policies; a study of student practice in selecting H&SS courses; and the identification of programs exemplifying some promising approaches to the challenge of providing, within the severe constraints of the engineering curriculum, an H&SS experience of value.

In the pages that follow, we are pleased to share the results of this work. Chapter One explains the value of H&SS coursework and describes briefly some of the obstacles that confront efforts to improve it. Chapter Two summarizes the findings of two empirical studies of engineering programs' policies and of H&SS course selection. The third chapter briefly describes thirteen programs, or parts of programs, that provide liberal education to engineering students in ways that may spark thinking at other institutions in search of curricular ideas. With special attention to the situation at the "typical" engineering school, the fourth and final chapter suggests criteria for improving H&SS coursework and steps that can help create a climate and mechanisms to support that improvement. Finally, it provides several examples of H&SS components conforming to these criteria and constructed from courses available on most campuses.

This interim report is intended primarily for policy makers. It has been designed, that is, to assist those— national and professional leaders, central university adminstrators, deans and faculty members in engineering and the arts and sciences—who are in positions to influence either national or institutional policy with regard to H&SS coursework. A second and final project publication, coming later this year, is intended for engineering majors and their advisors. Drawing extensively on the conclusions of a project-funded working conference in October 1987, it will make the case for the value of H&SS coursework, urge closer attention to the planning of course selections, and suggest various H&SS course combinations likely to appeal to engineering students with different needs and interests. The project will conclude with a conference in September 1988 that will bring together interdisciplinary teams of engineering and liberal arts educators from institutions across the country. Its purpose will be to equip them as informed advocates, on their own campuses, of a more central role for liberal studies in undergraduate engineering education.

It is a pleasure to thank those who have contributed to this publication. The project has benefited at many points from the involvement and counsel of a distinguished advisory committee. While this report itself should not be construed as expressing a committee position, the committee's members speak with one voice on the importance of the problems discussed, and their perspectives are reflected here in many ways. The members of the advisory committee are:
☐ Joseph Bordogna, Dean, School of Engineering and Applied Science, University of Pennsylvania
☐ Edmund T. Cranch, Granite State Distinguished Professor of the University System of New Hampshire
☐ Samuel C. Florman, Vice President, Kreisler Borg Florman Construction Company
☐ O. Allan Gianniny, Jr., Professor of Humanities, School of Engineering and Applied Science, University of Virginia
☐ Margaret L. MacVicar, Dean for Undergraduate Education, Massachusetts Institute of Technology
☐ William F. Prokasy, Dean of Liberal Arts and Sciences, University of Illinois at Urbana-Champaign
☐ David Reyes-Guerra, Executive Director, Accreditation Board for Engineering and Technology
☐ Linda B. Salamon, Dean, College of Arts and Sciences, Washington University
☐ J. David Waugh, Professor of Engineering, University of South Carolina

AAC's work has been assisted at many points by the Accreditation Board for Engineering and Technology (ABET). We are particularly grateful to Russel Jones and David Reyes-Guerra, president and executive director of ABET, respectively, for their interest and support. We appreciate, as well, the interest of the Liberal Education Division of the American Society of Engineering Education (ASEE), which has devoted numerous annual meeting sessions to this project.

AAC's contractor for the transcript analysis presented in Chapter Two is the Institute for Research on Higher Education (IRHE) of the University of Pennsylvania. The institute's staff, under the direction of co-authors Robert Zemsky and Susan Shaman, tackled the project with creativity and skill, helping develop methods for understanding student coursework from transcript data that hold promise for other studies. Substantial contributions were made by Sandy Rosenberg, Venkat Gangisetty, Peter Zemsky, Dan Shapiro, James Cocroft, James Wamsley, and Greg Wegner.

I thank all those who provided

INTRODUCTION

information on the campus programs highlighted in Chapter Three. All sent written materials and gave telephone interviews with no assurance that their programs would ultimately be included. Their names appear at the end of the descriptions of their programs. Allan Gianniny, an advisory committee member, deserves special thanks for his help in researching and selecting the programs to be featured, and for assistance generously given throughout the project.

I am indebted to William LeBold of Purdue University for a substantial and helpful commissioned background paper that influenced this project's direction at the outset; to Lance Schachterle, professor of English and chair of the Division of Interdisciplinary Affairs at Worcester Polytechnic Institute, for his assistance in identifying thematic areas appropriate for H&SS study; to the incisive and comprehensive reports prepared during the last three years at the Massachusetts Institute of Technology by three faculty committees—the Humanities, Arts and Social Sciences Requirements (HASS) Committee; the School of Science and Education Committee; and the Commission on Engineering Undergraduate Education—and to several fine books by Samuel C. Florman, most notably *The Civilized Engineer* (St. Martin's Press, 1987). The MIT and Florman analyses have shaped the present work in ways too numerous to recount, and it draws extensively on their insights.

This report also owes much to the participants of the project's working conference of engineering and liberal arts educators held in October 1987. They include Tad Beckman, Harvey Mudd College; Melvin Cherno, Allan Gianniny, and Robert Kellogg, University of Virginia; Edmund Cranch, University System of New Hampshire; Edward Daub, University of Wisconsin; Richard Devon, Pennsylvania State University; William Grogan, Worcester Polytechnic Institute; Richard Jacobs, California State Polytechnic University–Pomona; Mark Levinson, University of Maine; W. David Lewis, Auburn University; Judith Liebman and William Prokasy, University of Illinois at Urbana-Champaign; Ernest Lynton, University of Massachusetts–Boston; Luz Martinez-Miranda and David Pope, University of Pennsylvania; Susan Resneck Parr and Y. T. Shaw, University of Tulsa; Thomas Phelan, Rensselaer Polytechnic Institute; Thomas Philipose, Colorado School of Mines; David Reyes-Guerra, Accreditation Board for Engineering and Technology; Linda Salamon, Washington University; James Schaub, University of Florida; and Lambert Van Poolen, Calvin College.

As mentioned above, the work of these participants will be featured more fully in a forthcoming booklet for engineering students and their advisors. This report, however, draws on the effective work of three subgroups in particular, led by Susan Resneck Parr, Lambert Van Poolen, and Linda Salamon.

It is owing largely to the leadership of AAC President John W. Chandler that this project was begun, and he has provided guidance and support throughout. AAC's Matthew Anderson contributed extensively, providing able processing support for the survey of institutional policies. I am indebted as well to other colleagues, including Carol Schneider, Harry Smith, Sherry Levy-Reiner, Lauran Nohe, Karen Poremski, Jane Spalding, Shelagh Casey, and David Stearman, for many different forms of assistance. Special thanks are due to Nora Topalian for her hard work and great patience in preparing the manuscript.

Finally, on behalf of AAC, I want to thank the Andrew W. Mellon Foundation and the Pew Memorial Trust. That both liberal arts and engineering educators have so extensively joined forces within AAC's project suggests its timeliness and importance. But it proves as well the power of effective philanthropy to focus concern and effort and make possible needed change.

—JOSEPH S. JOHNSTON, JR.

CHAPTER ONE

UNFINISHED DESIGN

THE RATIONALE FOR LIBERAL EDUCATION

DIMENSIONS OF THE PROBLEM

Most of us are familiar with Hamlet's phrase, "hoist with his own petar." Few, of us, however, can readily explain what a petar, or petard, is. We tend to assume that it is a hoist, or a crane, or a mast on a boat, perhaps some kind of spear or standard. Still fewer of us recall *who* it is that Hamlet imagines being hoisted by a petard (defined "as an explosive device formerly used to blow in a door or gate, form a breach in a wall, etc."). The answer is "the engineer," who in Hamlet's lines (III, iv, 213-214) makes his first appearance by that name in literature. This unpromising debut comes to mind now, when there is widespread and growing concern that today's and tomorrow's engineers not be hoisted by their own petards—victimized, that is, by the very academic specialization that assures them their technical expertise.

In many respects, the effectiveness of this country's system of engineering education is beyond dispute. The accomplishments of its graduates are legion. Transportation, sanitation, defense, health care, communication, building construction, space exploration, manufacturing, computing, water supply: It is difficult to think of an area of societal need to which engineers have not responded with competence and ingenuity.[1]

Consistently in demand by industry, engineers have for decades enjoyed an unemployment rate of no more than 2 percent.[2] They hold their share of top management positions,[3] they are the highest-paid salaried professionals,[4] and the vast majority report themselves quite satisfied with their working lives.[5]

Engineering educators can take pride not only in the success and accomplishments of those they have already trained but in the numbers and in the promise of those they are now preparing for the profession. Engineering enrollments are large and until recently have been growing steadily. By 1984, engineering degrees, as a proportion of all U.S. baccalaureate degrees awarded, reached 10 percent—up from 5 percent only a decade before.[6]

The one hundred thousand new students now entering these programs each year are typically bright and high achieving.[7] Their numbers include a growing percentage of the nation's ablest high school graduates—whose enrollment strengthens an already strong pool.[8] A recent study of a million students who took the Scholastic Aptitude Test over the last decade found that the cohort intending to enter engineering was, of twenty cohorts studied, eleventh in mean verbal scores, tenth in educational aspirations, fourth in high school rank and third in mean quantitative score.[9] (Engineering schools being relatively selective, the ranking of students actually accepted into their programs would be higher still.) Other studies tell us that today's engineering students represent a broader range of socioeconomic backgrounds than their predecessors, and that they are more likely as high school students to have had a range of extracurricular involvements.[10] These are clearly young people whose interests, abilities, and aspirations will propel them in large numbers into management and leadership positions, some of a kind seldom held or sought by engineers before.

The practical effectiveness of an engineering education, seen both in the accomplishments of engineering graduates and in the size and quality of current enrollments, is not an accident. Appropriately for the field of engineering, it is the product of careful design. Not only university faculty and administrators but numerous government agencies, professional societies, industrial and educational associations, foundations, academies, and other national organizations make engineering education the focus of their study and support. Because the baccalaureate-level degree in engineering is the standard professional credential, these individuals and organizations have focused particular attention on the undergraduate curriculum. The course of study that they have developed is carefully planned. It is also more highly structured, and more directive in its specific requirements, than any other in undergraduate higher education. This curriculum is admirably efficient in providing requisite work in mathematics, science, and engineering science and design and in producing within four to five years employable, technically competent graduates. In this important sense, the undergraduate engineering curriculum is a particularly successful design.

The concern that prompts our project, however, is that undergraduate engineering education is not effective enough. Continuing improvements in the teaching of science, mathematics, and engineering alone, moreover, cannot solve the problem, as essential as these improvements are to maintaining quality. Another area of the engineering curriculum must be reformed, one that is by contrast neglected and seriously in disarray. We refer to the humanities and the social sciences. More thought must be given to engineers' very limited coursework in these areas, and steps must be taken to ensure its quality. Until this happens, for all its strengths, the undergraduate engineering education will remain an unfinished design.

THE RATIONALE FOR LIBERAL EDUCATION

The pages that follow present new evidence that humanities and social science coursework—the liberal studies or "H&SS" component as it is widely known in engineering education—needs attention. They also suggest steps to improve it. First, though, the question can fairly be asked why there is an H&SS component in the first place. What, briefly, is the rationale for liberal studies?

Frank Rhodes of Cornell University has warned of the "alarming gap between the pretensions and the performance of the liberal arts." Clearly the influence of studying these fields can be overstated. The quality of particular offerings varies enormously, and even the best of them have no patent on the provision of liberal education. Engineers know all this as well as anyone (and are perhaps readier than most to point it out), yet liberal arts coursework has, as a matter of policy, long been a fixture of the engineer's undergraduate experience.

At some level, this tradition recognizes a liberal education's broadest values. One is a human being first and an engineer second. To be human is to encounter realms of experience in which scientific and technological paradigms simply do not work.[11] Liberal learning equips the engineer with ways of thinking that complement those driven home within the engineering school's powerfully pragmatic and quantitative culture. Taught well, it is generally thought, the liberal arts help equip us for citizenship, for family, for productive intercourse of all sorts. They transmit culture, history, tradition—in Samuel Florman's words, "the shared knowledge and values that bind us together as a society."[12] At the same time, they can sharpen our critical powers and help us examine our preconceptions. A strong liberal education, in

As we approach and enter the twenty-first century, technology will give all engineers a still more central role in society

short, promotes qualities—a breadth of curiosity, reference, and understanding; flexibility; critical thinking; an ability to learn—that serve one well in any career and over a lifetime. It can help make us what we are capable of becoming and provide personal enrichment and pleasures that are their own rewards.

Explanations of the place accorded the liberal arts within engineering education often make less of these broad benefits, however, than of those that serve engineers as engineers. "Studies in the humanities and social sciences," asserts the professional accrediting agency, "... meet the objectives of the engineering profession."[13]

At a very pragmatic level, this line of argument holds, liberal learning helps develop decision making and other skills needed for good engineering design. It can exercise engineers' imaginations in ways that foster intuition and creativity. It helps them deal with issues—for example, what problems are to be solved, how specifications are to be written, what materials and energy sources are to be used—that, though practical, transcend engineering science.

Liberal study is also widely valued as a way of developing skills of clear, persuasive communication. These skills are essential at a time when engineering is more a group enterprise and team effort than ever, and when engineers must increasingly explain their work to nonengineers—consumers, legislators, judges, bureaucrats, environmentalists, and members of the press—in order to achieve their professional aims.[14]

Many technical problems are also social problems—or ethical, or political, or international problems—and some ability to confront them as such is also an increasingly necessary part of the professional equipment of engineers.[15] Study of the humanities and social sciences can help, alerting future engineers to the contexts of their work and fostering thoughtfulness about its consequences.

A good liberal education also provides engineers a foundation broad enough for professional growth. It reduces their chances of becoming replaceable parts, or of suffering the fate of the actor described by Will Durant, who knew his role but was ignorant of the plot and the meaning of the play. More than this, however, a liberal education can help prepare engineers for careers in management, for public office, and for other forms of leadership. It is more widely recognized now than it was a few years ago that every liberal arts discipline—literature and philosophy no less than psychology and economics—has contributions to make to the development of effective managers. And Samuel Florman, among others, has made the case that liberally educated engineers should also be especially well equipped for public office and participation in society's "highest councils," where they might not only help ensure informed public decision making on technological issues but win increased public esteem and influence for their profession as well.[16]

These are more or less timeless arguments. There are also reasons why strengthening the role of liberal studies in engineering has growing influence today. One is that two-thirds of new tenure-track faculty appointments in engineering in U.S. universities now go to individuals who are born outside the U.S. Some of these foreign-born engineering faculty, of course, are broadly educated and have much to contribute to their students' liberal education. But many of them have, by their own admission, small acquaintance with liberal studies and little comprehension of its value. The ability of engineering faculty themselves to help impart the knowledge and the habits of thought traditionally associated with a liberal education can less and less be taken for granted. A proportionately greater responsibility for liberal education now falls to the arts and sciences.

There is another broad reason for thinking that liberal learning is an increasingly critical part of engineering education. As we approach and enter the twenty-first century, technology will give all engineers a still more central role in society. We have already mentioned that today's best engineering students will rise to positions of leadership and power in unprecedented numbers. But in a smaller, more technological world—a world more dependent than ever on systems and products that are safe, environmentally sound, and socially beneficial—more typical engineers, too, will shoulder new responsibilities for the public good. Their responsibilities may not be entirely welcome. But to meet them, these engineers will need as broad a range of intellectual skills and understanding as they can summon.

Other benefits are claimed and other reasons given for liberal learning. A full list would contain some that are fanciful. It would include many that have been made in lip service. But the truth of the essential argument is clear both to lay persons and thoughtful engineering educators. It is not enough that tomorrow's engineers be well trained; they must also be well educated. The effective program will embrace liberal education not as an afterthought but as a vital component of professional study.

DIMENSIONS OF THE PROBLEM

How many schools would measure up to criteria of program effectiveness that put serious weight on the size, quality, and coherence of the H&SS component? Good data are scarce, but anecdotal evidence and a number of limited studies suggest that the answer is "too few."

First, although a broad foundation in the liberal arts is essential for engineering students, no group of undergraduates seems to encounter liberal arts disciplines less. U.S. Department of Education researchers who recently analyzed a sample of engineering transcripts as part of a more general analysis of undergraduate coursework, found that engineers take only 9 percent of their work in the humanities (including composition courses). This figure compares with 12 to 67 percent taken by majors in other fields. In the social sciences, engineers again take 9 percent, compared with 13 to 22 percent taken by their peers.[17]

Just as worrisome as the limited scope of engineers' H&SS coursework is its reputed lack of balance and coherence. A variety of reports have identified prevailing approaches to course selection. One approach is to meet the H&SS requirement with as many courses in the "practical" social sciences—and as few courses in the humanities—as possible. Another is to take a more or less random set of introductory courses. A third is simply to choose courses by their times, their locations, and the alleged ease of their instructors' grading—often with a preference for the courses likeliest to provide a respite from the engineer's "real work" (and hence not seen as calling for serious enquiry).[18] Obviously many engineering students make good use of their H&SS courses. But followed singly or in combination, strategies like these waste a very limited opportunity. They lead to liberal arts coursework that fails to serve any notion of general education or indeed add up to any meaningful educational experience at all.

Some key causes of the problem are known. One is the limited time available within engineering's nominally four-year curriculum, which already takes an average of 4.5 to 4.8 years to complete.[19] The Accreditation Board for Engineering and Technology (ABET) requires that a minimum of 12.5 percent, or one semester, of a student's coursework be in the H&SS area.[20] Although this is the least extensive liberal arts requirement by any accrediting agency, requirements in mathematics, science, and engineering sciences have helped, in many cases, to make this minimum an effective maximum.

An expanded five- or six-year curriculum is an obvious alternative, and one strongly recommended in some quarters. For a variety of reasons, however, most experiments in this direction have failed. There also seems little prospect at present of ABET's reserving substantially more time for H&SS in the standard engineering curriculum. Indeed, one concern now—when demands are heard for more science, more math, more practice-oriented coursework—is to preserve the current requirement.

Limited time is only one difficulty, however. Another is the widespread failure of engineering programs to demand structure or coherence of their students' H&SS coursework and to spell out their expectations in policies that elaborate on ABET's very broad prescriptions. This in turn often reflects the attitudes of engineering faculty who, though charged by ABET with ultimate responsibility for advising, tend to know little about the liberal arts. Too many regard H&SS coursework with indifference or think of it as a trivial and unnecessary part of the engineering program—and in any case someone else's responsibility.[21] Liberal arts faculty have, for their part, shown little interest in meeting their engineering colleagues halfway. The two groups have been most united in their common neglect of the H&SS component.

As with most complex problems, there is blame enough to be shared on all sides. What is most needed, however, is a constructive response. Fortunately, with the widespread computerization of transcript records, we can now document some of the dimensions of the problem—itself a matter of some controversy. We can also identify both a number of programs that have taken steps to improve H&SS coursework and some of the key considerations to be borne in mind by those in other institutions who want to set about that task.

This publication is designed for these purposes. Chapter Two reports on AAC's recent analyses both of what engineering programs currently require in H&SS and of what their students actually take. Chapter Three provides descriptions of selected programs that have already been undertaken to improve H&SS coursework. Chapter Four concludes this report with a set of recommendations to programs considering future reforms.

CHAPTER TWO

AN ANALYSIS: PROGRAM POLICY AND STUDENT PRACTICE

ENGINEERING PROGRAM POLICY
ON H&SS COURSEWORK

STUDENT PRACTICE IN SELECTING COURSES

In this chapter we examine the undergraduate engineering curriculum from two perspectives:
☐ by analyzing the policies through which engineering programs influence the course-taking of their students; and
☐ by examining the actual practice of engineering students in selecting courses. The focus of both investigations is on the humanities and social sciences—or H&SS—component of the curriculum.

Both program policy and student practice as described here should be compared with national policy as it is expressed in the key criteria for H&SS coursework promulgated by ABET. These criteria are established by ABET's board of directors, which is composed of representatives of twenty-four major technical and professional engineering societies. ABET conducts direct on-site visits in an effort to ensure compliance with all its criteria, including those related to H&SS coursework.

First, for ABET's purposes and ours, an H&SS course may be:
☐ a traditional, free-standing offering within the broad areas of the humanities (including foreign languages and certain nonperforming or nonstudio-

The orientation of certain courses toward one or another area often depends, of course, on the faculty at a particular institution

based arts courses) or the social sciences, and
□ an interdisciplinary offering that combines the perspectives of the humanities and the social sciences or of engineering with one or both of these.

An H&SS course may *not* be:
□ a course in a business discipline or military training, and
□ primarily designed to impart skills—for example, in written or oral communication.

As of the academic year 1986–87, the essential ABET requirements governing the H&SS component of an undergraduate engineer's education were that it:
□ constitute a minimum of 12.5 percent—about one semester's worth, or sixteen credit hours—of the student's total program;
□ "be planned to reflect a rationale or fulfill an objective appropriate to the engineering profession and the institution's educational objectives"; and
□ include "some courses at an advanced level rather than be limited to a selection of unrelated introductory courses."[22]

ABET provides little or no further detail and it leaves to individual program administrators the task of implementing these few general prescriptions. Engineering educators, in short, are given considerable discretion for policy making in the H&SS area. The first concern of our analysis has been to determine what they do with it.

ENGINEERING PROGRAM POLICY ON H&SS COURSEWORK

□ *Method.* The source of our data on engineering programs' policies is a survey questionnaire sent by AAC in the summer of 1986 to all 285 institutions that then had ABET-accredited engineering programs. Two hundred and four of these institutions (71.6 percent) returned the questionnaire. At our request, survey recipients also shared the relevant portions of their catalogues and other published guidelines. We resolved ambiguities in the completed surveys by contacting the respondents directly.

Responding institutions reflect the diversity within ABET: They range from small colleges with engineering departments to technical institutes to major universities in which engineering constitutes one of a number of distinct schools, and from those that teach only a few engineering undergraduates to those with extensive graduate as well as undergraduate programs. While the survey addressed a number of different issues, it focused on stated requirements regarding H&SS coursework.

We use three separate sets of terms to report on our results. The first set of terms classifies courses into four areas of study that together constitute H&SS as ABET defines it: humanities, social sciences, arts, and interdisci-

AN ANALYSIS:
PROGRAM POLICY
AND
STUDENT PRACTICE

plinary studies. (For clarity, all references in this chapter to the aggregate will be to "H&SS"; the four discrete areas of study will be referred to in the fashion just used.)

The orientation of certain courses toward one or another area often depends, of course, on the faculty at a particular institution. When it is provided, we use each institution's definition of the area to which a particular course belongs. Unless treated otherwise by the institution, we classify history as a humanities discipline and psychology as a social science. Courses that explicitly combine the perspectives of the humanities and social sciences are classified as "interdisciplinary." So are those that combine one or both of these perspectives with that of engineering (as do, for instance, the widely offered courses known generally as "Science, Technology, and Society").

The second set of terms provides the two basic measures we use to describe the H&SS component: breadth and depth. As indicated above, the ABET criteria require that students' programs of study include "some courses at an advanced level"—clearly, a "depth" requirement. They specify no requisite number of advanced courses, however, and provide no definition of an "advanced" course. Moreover, ABET makes no mention of any form of breadth, either across the humanities and the social sciences

or within either of these two areas. In the absence of a comprehensive and detailed set of appropriate measures from ABET, we developed a set specifically for this study. Our measures focus on the number of courses taken and the breadth and depth of coverage these courses represent. In this respect, the measures reflect attributes of coursework that have historically been the focus of most college and university distribution requirements.

It is important to note that our definitions of these measures are minimal ones. That is, they set extremely low thresholds for the achievement of breadth and depth—indeed, arguably lower in the case of depth than that implicit in ABET's own criteria. To use more demanding definitions, however, would be to obscure the limited amount of breadth and depth that engineering graduates actually achieve in their H&SS work.

We classify a program as requiring "breadth across areas" if it requires students to take at least one humanities course and at least one social sciences course. "Breadth across areas" could measure equally well coursework in the area of the arts or interdisciplinary studies together, or in combination with one of those other two; because the humanities and social sciences are the principle H&SS areas, however, our focus here and elsewhere is upon them.

UNFINISHED
DESIGN

Similarly, any school that mandates at least one course in each of two disciplines within the humanities or within the social sciences we consider to require "breadth *within* (that area)." A requirement, for example, that students study both English literature and philosophy is a requirement of breadth within the humanities.

In our discussion of program policy, "depth" simply refers to a requirement that students take at least one advanced course in a particular discipline. We treat as an advanced offering any course identified as such by the institution—usually by its being listed as fulfilling a requirement of advanced work or as having certain prerequisites.

A third and final set of terms describes each program's policy with respect to our measures. This is necessary because while some programs are very prescriptive with regard to H&SS coursework, others allow students considerable latitude. Some, for example, simply present their students with a long list of "acceptable" H&SS

FIGURE 1
PROGRAM POLICY
NUMBER OF H&SS COURSES REQUIRED
(204 PROGRAMS SURVEYED)

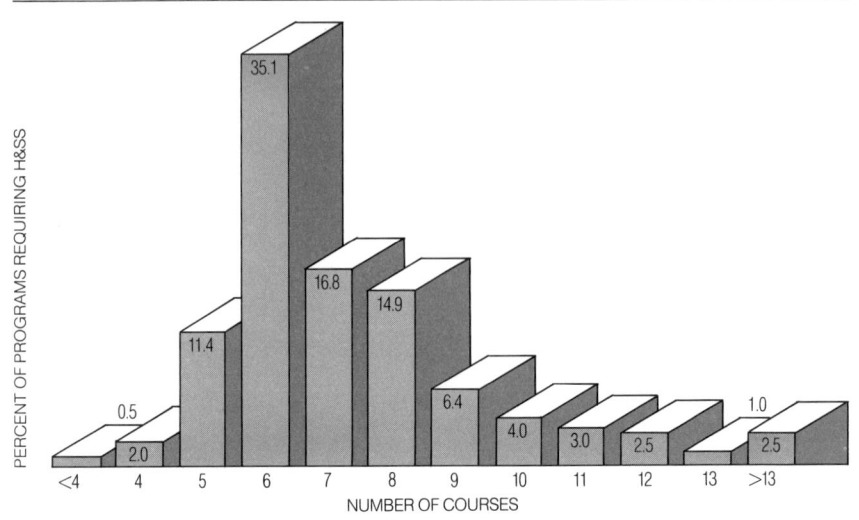

AN ANALYSIS:
PROGRAM POLICY
AND
STUDENT PRACTICE

courses and invite them to select any ones they wish. Other programs present guidelines that point, but still do not force, students toward certain choices.

The first of the four terms we use to describe this dimension of each program's policy is "required." This term denotes a program's setting forth clear instructions compelling students to meet certain criteria. For example, a program that compels students to take both introductory economics and an advanced economics elective requires depth in the social sciences.

If a program mandates that students take both economics and political science courses, breadth within the social sciences is required.

We use the term "available" to describe the more common instance in which a program's guidelines allow, or encourage, students to meet certain criteria. Where breadth or depth is available, nothing in the guidelines explicitly compels students to achieve depth or breadth, and students can in fact easily circumvent any institutional intention that they

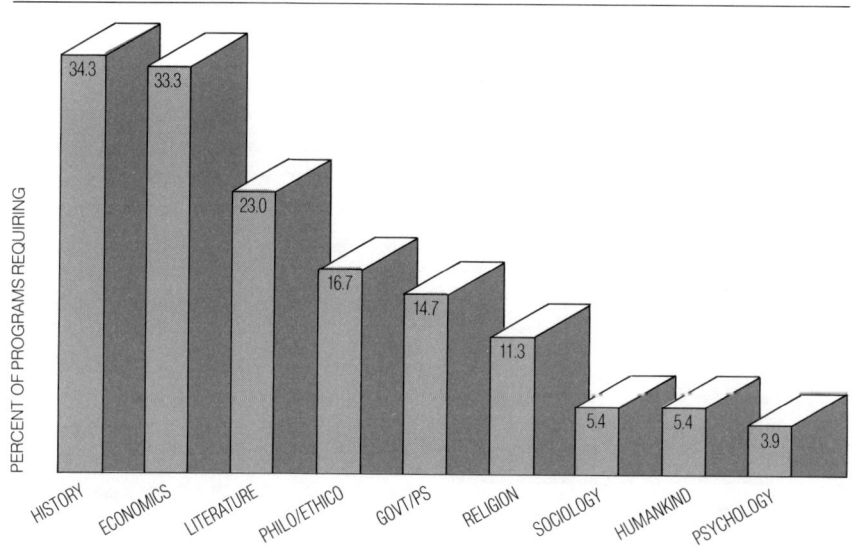

FIGURE 2
PROGRAM POLICY
H&SS DISCIPLINES WITH REQUIRED COURSES
(204 PROGRAMS SURVEYED)

UNFINISHED DESIGN

do so. For example, a program requiring "Introduction to Western Philosophy," and either "Introduction to Eastern Philosophy" or an advanced philosophy course would ensure that depth in the humanities is "available," but not "required." Similarly, if students must choose two courses from a pool consisting of English 201, English 207, History 103, History 403, History 319, Linguistics 107, and Linguistics 108, breadth within the humanities is at most available.

Two additional circumstances we denote as "discouraged" and "impossible." "Discouraged" describes a situation in which curricular restrictions make it difficult for students to meet certain criteria. "Impossible" signifies cases in which a narrow set of requirements actually precludes their doing so. For example, a school that requires specific courses in religion, economics, and music might, by doing so, prevent students from achieving depth or breadth within the social sciences or humanities. (It should be remembered that, for purposes of this analysis, the humanities and the arts are separate areas).

The H&SS requirements of programs are, of course, influenced by the policies of the engineering schools and the institutions in which they reside. We do not, however, distinguish the different levels from which particular requirements come, nor do we trace their interaction. A program policy, for present purposes, is a "student's-eye" view of H&SS requirements, whatever their source, within a particular engineering program.

Finally, if policies vary significantly among a responding institution's different engineering programs, we use a program identified by the institution as typical in its H&SS requirements. In cases in which we lack even that information, we use electrical engineering requirements as the basis

FIGURE 3
PROGRAM POLICY
BREADTH ACROSS HUMANITIES AND SOCIAL SCIENCES
(204 PROGRAMS SURVEYED)

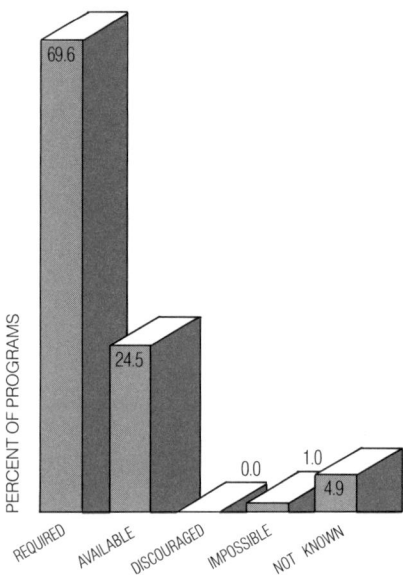

AN ANALYSIS: PROGRAM POLICY AND STUDENT PRACTICE

for our analysis.

□ *Findings.* Before reporting the breadth and depth policies of the programs surveyed, we present overviews of the amount of coursework required and the various areas in which these courses fall. Figure 1 shows the total numbers of H&SS courses required by respondents (a "course," our standard unit of measure, in most cases equals three semester hours of credit). Figure 2 displays the particular disciplines in which H&SS work is most frequently required.

Figure 1 shows that nearly 90 percent of the programs in our survey require between five and ten courses in H&SS. The modal number of required courses is six—with more than one-third of programs reporting that number. Given that most engineering programs in our survey consist of forty to forty-eight courses or their equivalent, it is clear that most of them also satisfy ABET guidelines as to the overall size of the H&SS component.

Some—though not all—surveyed programs require particular courses, or at least courses in particular disciplines. In Figure 2, we display the disciplines in which work is most frequently required. Any discipline required by at least five different programs appears on this graph. A program that compels students to select among courses in a given discipline or to take a specific course (or courses) counts as a "requiring" school on the vertical axis. Thus, more than one-third of the programs we studied require students to take a particular history course or enroll in a history course of their own choosing; one-third require some economics; and slightly less than a quarter require work in literature. (The label "Humankind" [Humkd] on this figure applies to any interdisciplinary course that involves human interaction with technology, machinery, or science.)

Clearly, there is little agreement among engineering programs about

FIGURE 4
PROGRAM POLICY
BREADTH WITHIN HUMANITIES
(204 PROGRAMS SURVEYED)

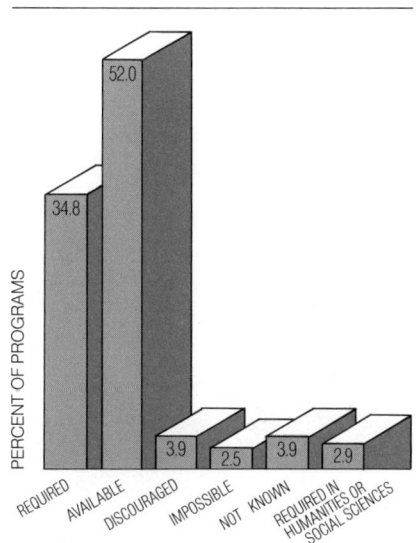

While breadth across the humanities and social sciences is usually required and almost always possible, breadth within these areas is less frequently required and occasionally difficult or impossible to obtain

which specific H&SS disciplines students should study. The figure shows that no area was required by even a majority of the programs surveyed. (It is important to recall here that "requiring" programs are defined as those that explicitly require enrollment in a particular subject. This means that virtually all students in the programs treated here as requiring history [the 34.3 percent displayed] will have enrolled in a history course. It also means, however, that there are institutions excluded from this set that offer history, for example, as one of a group of disciplines in which a requirement can be met.)

Figure 2 also shows, however, that when engineering programs do require coursework, they are more likely to mandate that it be in the humanities than in the social sciences. This finding reflects in some cases the influence of institution-wide general education requirements. In others, it may reflect a concern that, left to choose their H&SS courses freely, many engineers would take virtually all of them in the social sciences.

Figures 3 through 9 illustrate the policies of the surveyed programs concerning the breadth and depth of H&SS coursework. Figure 3 examines the policy of requiring students to achieve "breadth across areas"—in this case, to take at least one course in the humanities and one in the social sciences (again, the areas of the arts and interdisciplinary studies, in which relatively few courses are taken, are not considered here). The courses may be completely prescribed, or they may be chosen by the student. In either event, more than two-thirds of the programs ensure by the construction of their requirements that students take at least one course in the humanities and one in the social sciences. Skeptics will note that more than one quarter do not. Nearly all

FIGURE 5
PROGRAM POLICY
BREADTH WITHIN SOCIAL SCIENCES
(204 PROGRAMS SURVEYED)

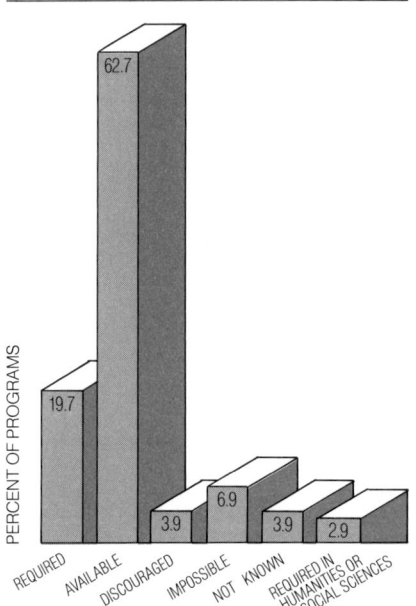

of the remaining programs, however, have policies that *allow* their students to take at least one course in both the humanities and social sciences. Very few have requirements that make breadth across these areas impossible.

While breadth across the humanities and social sciences is usually required and almost always possible, breadth within these areas is less frequently required and occasionally difficult or impossible to obtain. Figure 4 shows that slightly more than one-third of the programs surveyed require their students to take courses in at least two different disciplines within the humanities. More than half of the schools simply make available the option to study more than one humanities discipline, and more than 6 percent make it difficult or impossible for students to do so. Only 3 percent require some breadth within either the humanities or the social sciences.

As Figure 5 shows, policies with respect to the social sciences are still less prescriptive. Fewer than 20 percent of the surveyed programs require engineering students to study more than one discipline within the social sciences. While more than 60 percent allow students to study two or more social sciences, more than 10 percent discourage or prevent students' doing so. All these findings are consistent with Figure 2, which shows that engineering programs more frequently require coursework in humanities disciplines than in the social sciences.

Figure 6 combines the breadth policies for the humanities and social sciences to illustrate in one grid how programs approach both areas. The figure shows that only a small proportion of them (27 out of the 196 on which we have relevent information) require students to explore more than one discipline in both humanities and social sciences. In ninety-four cases students can achieve breadth in both areas but are not explicitly required to do so in either. Surpris-

FIGURE 6
PROGRAM POLICY
SUMMARY: BREADTH WITHIN HUMANITIES AND SOCIAL SCIENCES
(204 PROGRAMS SURVEYED)

BREADTH WITHIN HUMANITIES				
IMPOSSIBLE	2	1	0	2
DISCOURAGED	1	1	5	1
AVAILABLE	10	94	0	2
REQUIRED	27 +6 in either	32	3	9
	REQUIRED	AVAILABLE	DISCOURAGED	IMPOSSIBLE

BREADTH WITHIN SOCIAL SCIENCES

ingly, eight programs (those in the upper right quadrant) make it difficult or impossible to achieve breadth in either area.

The patterns that emerge from our analysis of depth (defined as the taking of at least one course at an advanced level) are remarkably similar to those exhibited in our study of breadth. Programs appear, however, to be even less prescriptive about depth than about breadth. Figure 7 shows that fewer than one-fourth of our sample require any advanced coursework within the humanities, although nearly 45 percent make it available. Almost 9 percent of the programs make it difficult or impossible for students to do advanced work in the humanities. On the other hand, 20 percent of the programs require some advanced work in either the humanities or social sciences. Presumably, many of these programs have no restrictions preventing students from doing advanced work in both areas.

Fewer than 15 percent of the pro-

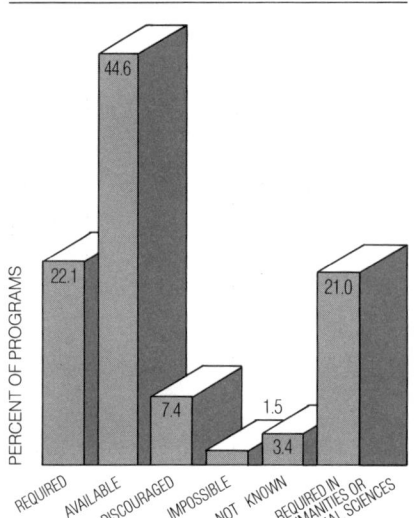

FIGURE 7
PROGRAM POLICY
DEPTH WITHIN HUMANITIES
(204 PROGRAMS SURVEYED)

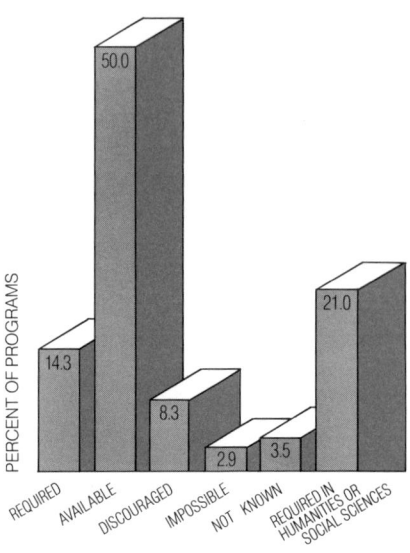

FIGURE 8
PROGRAM POLICY
DEPTH WITHIN SOCIAL SCIENCES
(204 PROGRAMS SURVEYED)

AN ANALYSIS:
PROGRAM POLICY
AND
STUDENT PRACTICE

grams explicitly require depth in the social sciences (Figure 8). Half make it possible, and more than 11 percent make it difficult or impossible to achieve. Again, that 21 percent of programs requiring advanced work in either the humanities or the social sciences also will have students who achieve depth in the social sciences. Finally, Figure 9 illustrates that only twenty-four programs—a comparatively small number—require advanced work in both the humanities and the social sciences. On the other hand, forty-three require some advanced work in either the humanities or the social sciences, and eighty-eight make it possible for students to do advanced work in both areas. In fourteen programs any advanced work in the humanities or social sciences is discouraged or impossible.

Several conclusions about program policies emerge from these survey results. First, a few programs actually fail to require H&SS courses in sufficient numbers to meet ABET standards. A large majority, however, do meet the standard, including a number that require H&SS components more extensive than the minimum one ABET suggests.

Second, many engineering programs do not prescribe particular H&SS coursework for their students, but tend instead to permit their students latitude within some sort of framework. Most institutions do ensure that their students achieve breadth across areas by requiring at least one course in both the humanities and the social sciences. Policies in a large proportion of institutions also enable—although they infrequently require—students to achieve breadth and depth within the humanities and social sciences.

Third, when specific requirements are established, they more often mandate work in the humanities than in the social sciences. In both the humanities and the social sciences, program policy more often promotes breadth than depth.

FIGURE 9
PROGRAM POLICY
SUMMARY: DEPTH WITHIN HUMANITIES AND SOCIAL SCIENCES
(204 PROGRAMS SURVEYED)

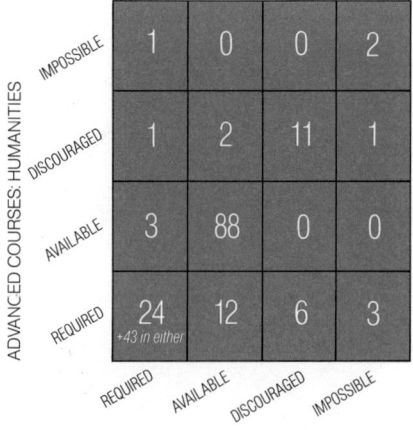

ADVANCED COURSES: SOCIAL SCIENCES

UNFINISHED DESIGN

STUDENT PRACTICE IN SELECTING COURSES

As ABET policy leaves much discretion to the engineering programs, so, then, do the policies of the programs leave considerable discretion to their students. The remainder of this analysis focuses on actual student practice in selecting H&SS courses—the results with which engineering majors exercise their freedom.

☐ *Method.* To determine the enrollment practices of engineering students, we obtained and analyzed the transcripts of a large sample of students enrolled in eighteen institutions. We first collected and examined the transcripts of all students who, in the spring of 1986, graduated with a major in business, the arts and sciences, or engineering from a sample group of eighteen colleges and universities. Using information about the curriculum derived from that first analysis as context, we then examined the engineers' transcripts in more detail.

The eighteen colleges and universities submitting transcripts were:

☐ California State University–Sacramento
☐ Colorado School of Mines
☐ Howard University
☐ Johns Hopkins University
☐ State University of New York–Stony Brook
☐ South Dakota School of Mines and Technology
☐ Stanford University
☐ Texas A&M University
☐ University of Illinois
☐ University of Maine
☐ University of Maryland–College Park
☐ University of North Dakota
☐ University of Pennsylvania
☐ University of South Carolina
☐ University of Virginia
☐ University of Tulsa
☐ Villanova University
☐ Washington University

Among these schools are seven public and eleven private institutions.

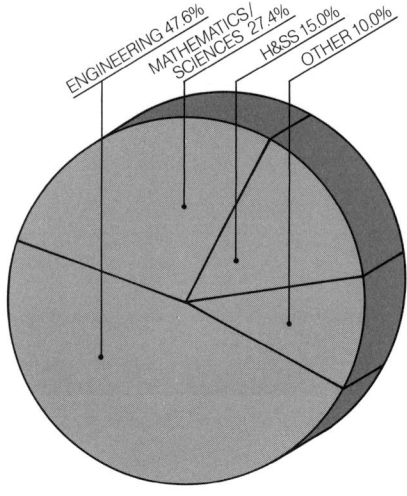

FIGURE 10
STUDENT PRACTICE
MEAN DISTRIBUTION OF ALL COURSEWORK
(ENGINEERING GRADUATES OF 18 INSTITUTIONS)

ENGINEERING 47.6% / MATHEMATICS/SCIENCES 27.4% / H&SS 15.0% / OTHER 10.0%

AN ANALYSIS:
PROGRAM POLICY
AND
STUDENT PRACTICE

Eleven of the eighteen are research universities, two are comprehensive institutions, and four—though smaller and less comprehensive—offer doctoral programs. Seven institutions in our sample are located in the Northeast, two in the South, four in the Midwest, and three in the West. As a whole, the sample is probably biased toward strong and selective engineering programs.

In four of the institutions, we analyzed only the transcripts of students who graduated within four years; in the other fourteen, where fewer than 85 percent of students graduate within that period, we analyzed those who graduated in five years as well. Since engineering students tend to enroll in H&SS courses predominantly in their first two years of study, we excluded transfer students from our analysis. The total number of engineering transcripts processed was 3,316.

The basic measures of student coursetaking employed in the previous section continue to figure in the present discussion but necessarily are defined somewhat differently in several cases. In this section, "breadth" continues to denote enrollment in two different disciplines within an area of study, either the humanities or the social sciences. "Depth" continues to describe enrollment in at least one advanced course. With transcript evidence at hand, however, we no longer depend on the institution's own designation to identify advanced courses. In the transcript analysis an advanced course is defined more descriptively than normatively as a course in which at least 75 percent of those enrolled have enrolled in a common prior course.

Several other small changes of method should be mentioned. In this transcript study we consistently classify history as belonging to the humanities and psychology as belonging to the social sciences. As before, following ABET dictates, we do not count speech, composition, and similar "skills"

FIGURE 11
STUDENT PRACTICE
MEAN DISTRIBUTION OF H&SS COURSEWORK
(ENGINEERING GRADUATES OF 18 INSTITUTIONS)

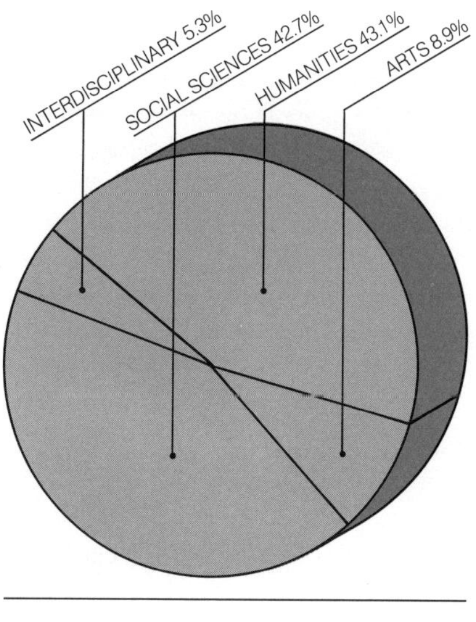

INTERDISCIPLINARY 5.3%
SOCIAL SCIENCES 42.7%
HUMANITIES 43.1%
ARTS 8.9%

UNFINISHED DESIGN

courses as humanities offerings. Here too, however, we have been able to consider factors other than a course's title in identifying its particular role. We assume—fairly, we think—that English courses with 75 percent or more of freshman enrollments are primarily writing or composition courses, even if literature based.

Finally, our concern in this analysis is with two sets of averages: the average student's experience with H&SS within a specific institution; and the average of this across all institutions—that is, an averaged average. The denominator in all calculations of the latter type is eighteen. We have *not* calculated weighted averages by enrollment.
□ *Findings.* Figure 10, the first of eight dealing with student practices, indicates how the average engineer's courses are distributed across several broad curricular areas. In the average institution, the typical student takes just under half of his or her coursework in the engineering sciences and design, a little more than a quarter in mathematics and the natural sciences, and 15 percent in H&SS. The remaining courses are for the most part communication skills courses (composition and speech) and courses in a professional school curriculum, principally business.

Figure 11 details the distribution of the average student's H&SS coursework. Despite—or perhaps because of—the fact that program policies more often require coursework in the humanities than in the social sciences, the two areas of study are nearly equal in their contribution. The relative absence of coursework in the arts is noteworthy. Most engineering students who earn degrees from the eighteen institutions we sampled graduate without taking any H&SS courses in this area.

Figure 12 displays the complete range of institutional averages. In most settings, the percentage of coursework in H&SS reflects ABET's policy that at least 12.5 percent be in these areas. At five institutions, however, students regularly graduate taking less. At two of the institutions graduating engineers devote, on the average, more than a quarter of their programs to H&SS courses. The institution with the greatest volume of H&SS coursework, one of the most selective in our sample, also has the most extensive core and distribution requirements in these areas. Its unusually heavy humanities enrollment may also result in part from the fact that this institution does not have an undergraduate business program.

The next four graphs focus on breadth and depth of courses taken by engineering students in the humanities and social sciences. In each of these, three separate distributions are plotted. The top line represents the experience of the institution providing the greatest breadth or depth

AN ANALYSIS:
PROGRAM POLICY
AND
STUDENT PRACTICE

FIGURE 12
STUDENT PRACTICE
H&SS COURSEWORK AS A PERCENT OF
ALL COURSEWORK
(ENGINEERING GRADUATES OF 18 INSTITUTIONS)

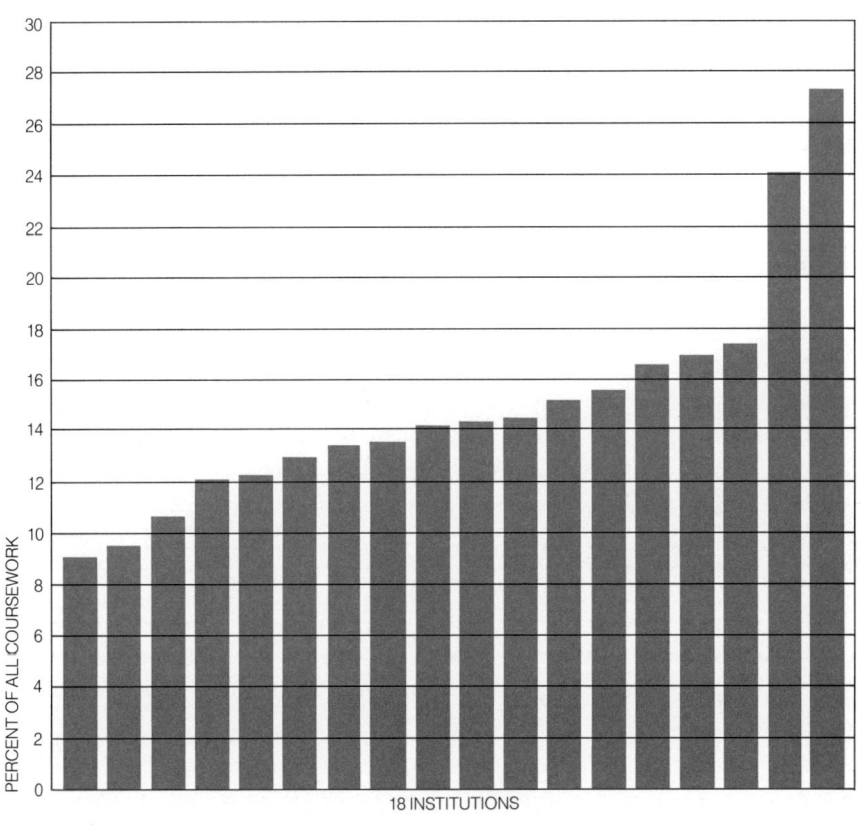

UNFINISHED
DESIGN

within the areas under consideration. The bottom line plots that of the institution providing the least. The middle line represents the average breadth or depth in the specified area across all eighteen institutions. The horizontal axis plots the number of separate disciplines in which courses are taken, while the vertical axis plots the cumulative percentage of graduating seniors.

Figure 13 shows, then, that almost all engineering graduates at the institution providing the greatest breadth within the humanities take at least one course in two separate humanities fields, just under 90 percent take courses in three, and more than half in four. On the other hand, at the institution providing the least breadth, fewer than half of the graduates take any humanities courses (excluding freshman English, composition, speech, and communications courses), and fewer than 10 percent take courses in two disciplines. No graduate of this institution takes courses in three separate humanities fields.

It is the middle line that best captures the average experience of students graduating from ABET-accredited institutions. Most, but not all, take at least one course in the humanities. Nearly 60 percent take courses in

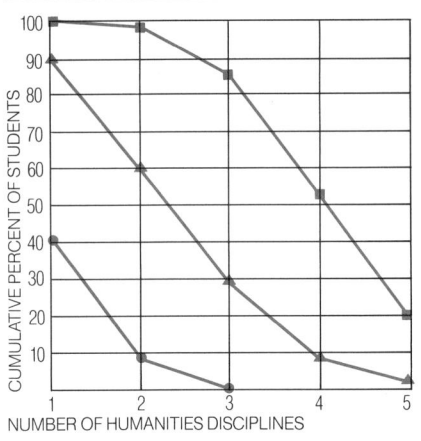

FIGURE 13
STUDENT PRACTICE
BREADTH WITHIN HUMANITIES
(ENGINEERING GRADUATES OF 18 INSTITUTIONS)

● MINIMUM BREADTH   ▲ MEAN BREADTH   ■ MAXIMUM BREADTH

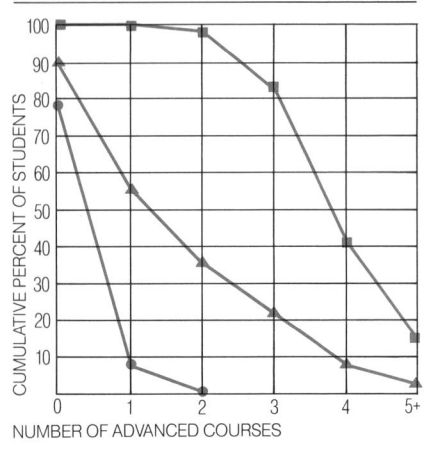

FIGURE 14
STUDENT PRACTICE
DEPTH WITHIN HUMANITIES
(ENGINEERING GRADUATES OF 18 INSTITUTIONS)

● MINIMUM BREADTH   ▲ MEAN BREADTH   ■ MAXIMUM BREADTH

AN ANALYSIS: PROGRAM POLICY AND STUDENT PRACTICE

two separate disciplines, though fewer than 30 percent take courses in three, and almost none in four. Thus, while students in a few institutions achieve considerable breadth in the humanities, most concentrate their humanities courses in just one or two fields.

Figure 14, plotting depth within the humanities, shows that this lack of breadth is not a function of advanced coursework. On the average, slightly more than half of engineering graduates take one advanced humanities course, and just a third take as many as two.

Figures 15 and 16, finally, plot breadth and depth within the social sciences. They show patterns of course selection that closely resemble, on the average, those reported for the humanities.

□ *Conclusions.* We began by noting that insofar as H&SS requirements and coursework are concerned, ABET grants considerable discretion to programs. We then found that programs, in turn, tend to give substantial latitude to their students. What, then, does our analysis of students' coursework tell us?

What is made of the H&SS opportunity varies enormously by student and institution. We have found, however, that students in most programs

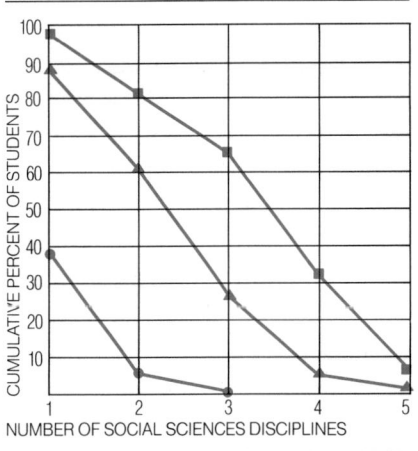

FIGURE 15
STUDENT PRACTICE
BREADTH WITHIN SOCIAL SCIENCES
(ENGINEERING GRADUATES OF 18 INSTITUTIONS)

● MINIMUM BREADTH   ▲ MEAN BREADTH   ■ MAXIMUM BREADTH

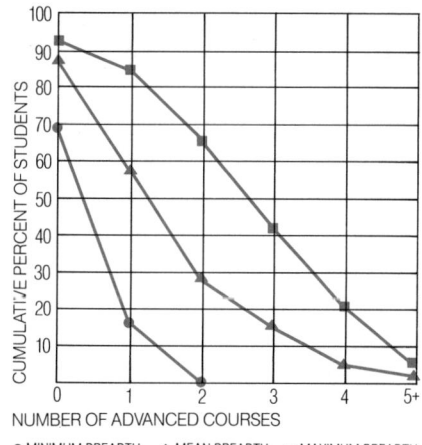

FIGURE 16
STUDENT PRACTICE
DEPTH WITHIN SOCIAL SCIENCES
(ENGINEERING GRADUATES OF 18 INSTITUTIONS)

● MINIMUM BREADTH   ▲ MEAN BREADTH   ■ MAXIMUM BREADTH

Many argue forcefully that, by meaningful definition of the terms, even minimal breadth and depth cannot be achieved within the semester's worth of coursework required as a minimum by ABET

take the required number of H&SS courses—though rarely many more. (They are more likely to achieve some breadth or depth [with 55 to 60 percent doing so at typical institutions] than their programs are to require that they do so.) This result, however, is to some extent predictable—even unavoidable—given five to eight course selections in a particular curricular area. The result depends, moreover, on necessarily minimal definitions of breadth and depth. As we have seen, the reported percentages would drop sharply if our definitions of these measures were more demanding.

It is often said that H&SS coursework not only lacks depth and breadth, but lacks thematic coherence as well.

FIGURE 17
TEN MOST FREQUENTLY TAKEN H&SS COURSES AT ONE INSTITUTION

INTRODUCTORY ECONOMICS
(FIRST SEMESTER)
INTRODUCTORY ECONOMICS
(SECOND SEMESTER)
INTRODUCTORY PSYCHOLOGY
THE FAMILY
RUSSIAN HISTORY
(SECOND SEMESTER)
LOGIC
SOCIAL STRATIFICATION
CLASSICAL TO MODERN MUSIC
ADVANCED ECONOMIC ANALYSIS
DEVIANTS AND SOCIAL CONTROL

Course titles and other forms of transcript evidence cannot by themselves prove or disprove this. Only educators on individual campuses, drawing on local knowledge of the content and approach of particular courses, can do so. The transcripts we examined, however, do suggest that the issue is an important one, for they exhibit less apparent coherence than one would hope.

The best term to describe the general course-taking patterns of engineering graduates in the humanities and social sciences would seem to be "episodic." We can give some content to this observation by listing the ten most frequently taken H&SS courses at one of our sample institutions (see Figure 17). The basic approach to course selection that this list reveals is characteristic of students at eleven of our eighteen institutions. It reflects the interaction of a largely laissez-faire H&SS policy, with the student course selection strategies already mentioned in Chapter One. A bias toward the purportedly more "useful" social sciences is clear. The institution in question has itself identified a number of these courses for us as relatively easily graded or taught by exceptionally popular lecturers. All these courses presumably have merit. But whether any five to eight of them that a given student might select would add up to something meaningful—making the H&SS component more than the sum of its parts—is unclear. Even all ten of these courses together would not appear to provide much of a general education.

These findings raise numerous questions for engineering educators at all levels. The most obvious is that of whether requirements—both ABET's and those of individual programs—are too lax or ill-defined. Certainly, we have seen that both ABET and individual engineering programs effectively shift to students considerable responsibility for their H&SS components and that this strategy has not resulted in the latter's taking significantly more courses than the minimum required or achieving much breadth or depth of coverage. There would seem to be ample room, and a real need, then, for more extensive, comprehensive and detailed H&SS requirements at both the ABET and program levels.

We have not traced the myriad interactions of institutional and program policies. Since the former so often shape the latter, however, policymakers at the college, university, and system levels must recognize their own responsibility for engineers' H&SS coursework. This is especially important in those cases where superficial, narrow or episodic H&SS coursework is in part an unintended result of a laissez-faire approach to general education requirements on the part of the institution as a whole. A policy of granting students relatively unrestricted freedom of choice may or may not have merit in the case of other undergraduates, but it seems clearly to work to the detriment of engineers. Their H&SS component affords them too little freedom for exploration and too little margin for error for it to be otherwise.

We conclude, in short, that much can be done at every level at which policy is now formulated—that of ABET, of institutions, and of individual engineering programs—to improve the quality of engineers' H&SS coursework. More effectively enforcing compliance with current criteria would by itself ensure progress. But these guidelines themselves need to be strengthened and clarified. Many argue forcefully that, by meaningful definition of the terms, even minimal breadth and depth cannot be achieved within the semester's worth of coursework required as a minimum by ABET. Whether or not this floor is raised, ABET, institutions, and programs can encourage a more extensive experience in H&SS. They can require, moreover, that this experience be more structured and coherent, and they can define more explicitly—if still broadly—the attributes of breadth, depth, and the like that will make it so. Not until these steps are taken, it seems to us, are either H&SS policies or H&SS practices likely to serve their intended purposes.

CHAPTER THREE

INNOVATIVE PROGRAMS

The general state of H&SS coursework clearly gives cause for concern. But, we should also remember Twain's words upon first hearing Wagner's music: "It's not as bad as it sounds."

That is true in the current case, thanks in part to the pioneering efforts of a minority of engineering educators on individual campuses across the country. These faculty and administrators have already developed a wide variety of responses to the challenge of providing engineering majors a liberal education. They have fashioned programs to fit virtually every kind of undergraduate engineering environment and a range of particular educational objectives.

The innovations include alternative general education offerings for engineers at Auburn, Florida, and Cal Poly–Pomona; a professional engineering core in H&SS at Virginia; a Western culture core at Stanford; fifth-year programs at Dartmouth and Rochester; arrangements fostering international experience at the University of Illinois at Urbana-Champaign; an honors program at Colorado School of Mines; a thoroughly recast curriculum at Worcester Polytechnic; and unusually extensive and well-structured distribution requirements at Harvey Mudd, MIT, and Calvin College. Some of these examples are well known; others are not. Some have proven their success over a period of a decade or more; others are just being implemented. They are not necessarily put forward here as model programs—and certainly not as definitive solutions. Collectively, however, they represent a range of possibilities and may prompt new thinking in environments where solutions are needed. Every program featured here is ABET-accredited.

The individuals mentioned in the following program descriptions are the first to point out that credit for the conception, development, and operation of these programs extends to many other colleagues, past and present. Space has not allowed us to acknowledge the latter by name. Nor has it allowed us to include all the worthy programs we would have wanted.

Finally, the programs featured may, for all their variety, strike some readers as having limited relevence to their own institutional circumstances. It is with the needs of these readers in mind that we present in Chapter Four some considerations and strategies that may be still more generally applicable.

AUBURN UNIVERSITY

Auburn University's Technology and Civilization program encompasses a year-long sequence of interdisciplinary courses providing freshmen an alternative way of meeting parts of their general education requirement. The Auburn program's focus on technology makes it a popular course among students intending to be engineering majors. And for such students, contends W. David Lewis, Hudson Professor of History and Engineering, that focus also makes good pedagogical sense.

Offered by Auburn's Department of History, the three quarter-long courses in the Technology and Civilization program provide an unusual overarching historical survey of the connections between technology and society. The first course, History 204, begins with prehistoric times and concludes with the late middle ages. It deals with such topics as the early use of tools; the gradual development of machinery in Greece and Rome; the growth of military and civil engineering; the emergence of writing, reckoning, and pictorial representation; and the early development of science in Greek, Islamic, and other ancient cultures.

History 205 brings the story to the end of the nineteenth century, and focuses on the backgrounds of the Industrial Revolution: the development of water and wind power in early modern Europe, movable type, particular industries (for example, glass- and iron-making), and various steam technologies including steamboats and steam locomotives.

History 206 is a more topically than chronologically organized overview of the late nineteenth and twentieth centuries. Here students learn, for example, about the automobile and aviation revolutions made possible by the internal combustion engine; the development of automation; the emergence of mass communications, photography, and motion pictures; the development of electricity and resultant goods and services; the development of atomic physics and the atom bomb, computers, and rocketry and space travel. "By the end of the course," says Lewis, who designed and teaches the sequence, "I like at least to get us on the moon."

Lewis stresses that despite its chronological sweep, Technology and Civilization does not concentrate narrowly on technology. Its purpose is "to probe the many connections between technology and other aspects of human development, art, religion, literature, politics, economic life, military institutions, social and cultural values, environmental issues, and so on." History 205, for example, traces the connections among the agricultural revolution, the increasing population growth and the urban dynamism of early modern Europe, and the impulses that produced the great cathedrals of the twelfth and thirteenth centuries. It relates the building technology that created the new Gothic style to changing Neoplatonic theological concepts, stressing the idea of Christ as the light of the world. It places the increasing use of mechanical devices, especially the mechanical clock, in the context of the growth of monasteries and the Christian emphasis in the dignity of creative work. And it emphasizes the connections among the development of the printing press, the Renaissance revival of classical learning, and the Protestant Reformation.

Approaching history via technology in this way has its limitations, says Lewis. For one thing, it precludes the kind of nontechnological breadth one can achieve in a more conventional course. But, he emphasizes, for teaching students who lack an interest in history, it is a proven and effective strategy. "Education is a lifelong process, and the key is motivation." When engineering students discover "that the things they have loved all their lives—tools, machines, electronic devices, and so on—have a history of their own and one that is connected to a rich texture of cultural phenomena," that discovery can spark in them an abiding interest in the past. Conventional college-level history courses, which tend not to provide engineering students this kind of bridge, risk merely confirming the indifference or distaste for the humanities that many of these students may already have developed in high school.

Comprising some of the most popular courses on the Auburn campus, Technology and Civilization may also be the largest program of its type in the world. Since it was inaugurated in 1971, the faculty teaching in it has increased to four members. Each quarter, these four teach a total of six sections with an average enrollment of two hundred students per section and two twenty-student honor sections. Freshmen intending to study engineering constitute the largest

UNFINISHED
DESIGN

single block of enrollments, always a third or more of the total. But no science background is assumed, and with the full approval of the engineering school the courses are always open to students from any discipline. This policy is intended to ensure, says Lewis, that all enrolled have the additional intellectual stimulation that studying with students from other programs can provide.

The development of the Auburn sequence was made possible in the early 1970s by a grant from the Callaway Foundation, while the later creation of the honors sequence was funded by a grant from the National Endowment for the Humanities. Plans for the honors sequence were drawn up over a year's time by an interdisciplinary committee of faculty members working with the advice of an outside consultant, a philosopher of science. The program has won favorable notice in several studies in the U.S. and abroad. Efforts are underway to create a graduate program in history and engineering that would provide faculty members for similar courses at other institutions.

Lewis points out that the availability of such generalists is critical to the future of interdisciplinary programs like Technology and Civilization. Staffing these courses can be difficult, as the number of faculty interested in teaching large broad surveys is limited. Nonetheless, he believes these courses should be offered and are especially appropriate for land-grant universities and technical institutes, which enroll large numbers of students whose interest in history "is latent rather than actual."

For more information, contact W. David Lewis, Hudson Professor of History and Engineering, Department of History, Auburn University, Auburn University, Ala. 36849-3501.

UNIVERSITY OF VIRGINIA

Undergraduates in the University of Virginia's School of Engineering and Applied Sciences take their humanities and social science courses in two distinctly different settings on the Charlottesville campus. Like engineering majors at most institutions, they take a number of humanities and social science courses (four to six on average) in their university's College of Arts and Sciences. They take at least four more of these courses, however, within the engineering school itself, in its Division of Humanities. This arrangement reflects both an unusual commitment on the part of the institution and the engineering school's uncommon care in distinguishing among the different purposes of H&SS coursework.

Melvin Cherno, the Joseph L. Vaughan Professor of Humanities and humanities division chair, explains that courses taken in the College of Arts and Sciences serve such traditional general education functions as providing personal enrichment, fostering civic responsibility, and transmitting a common culture. Courses taken in the engineering school's humanities division, by contrast, are intended as a "direct and integral part of students' professional education, providing them with skills and attitudes and understandings that are necessary to their future work as engineers." These courses are concerned especially with the relationship between technology and the world that produces it—"where engineering is coming from and what engineering affects." They encourage students to recognize the aesthetic, political, philosophical, and other sociocultural contexts of their future careers—the ways in which their profession will connect with other things. (A strong complementary focus in these courses on speaking and writing helps ensure that students will be able to articulate those connections to nonspecialists just as effectively as they communicate with their peers on narrowly technical issues.) Humanities division courses, in short, provide a humanities perspective on technological issues that supplements both students' technical majors and the still more humanities and social science-centered courses taken in the College of Arts and Sciences. And the university considers them as important to the engineering student's professional development as courses in mathematics, computing, and the sciences.

Four humanities division courses are required of each student. The first, "Language, Communication and the Technological Society," is essentially a one-semester freshman writing course. The student elects the second from approximately a dozen one-semester 200-level courses. These, Cherno explains, might be termed "interface" or "STS-type" offerings. They bear titles such as "Technology, Aggression and Peace"; "Man and Machine: Vision of Tyranny and Freedom in Nineteenth and Twentieth Century Literature"; "Religion and Technology"; and—of particular local appeal—"Thomas Jefferson's Interests in Science and Technology." The third and fourth required courses, "Western Technology and Culture" and "The Engineer in Society," are taken in the students' senior year. The first of these two one-semester offerings presents a historical perspective on the cultural contexts of technology in Western civilization; the second, Cherno says, explores "various kinds of valuing—social, institutional, scientific, intellectual, and personal—characteristic of professional work in engineering."

A year-long thesis project required in connection with these two courses provides an opportunity to evaluate the student as the project manager of a research effort on a straight engineering topic. The student's success, however, in relating the project to its cultural contexts—placing it in a history of human or societal need; explaining previous efforts at solving the problem; providing an impact analysis that identifies likely legal, cultural, and other consequences; and recommending actions that would need to be taken to win social acceptance—is equally important to the project's assessment.

The division does not encourage students to take more than four of its own offerings, preferring instead that they take the rest of their H&SS courses in the College of Arts and Sciences, where they have the experience of intellectual exchange with students majoring in other fields.

Virginia's provision of a humanities program within its school of engineering has analogues at many technical institutes, but it may be unique among comprehensive universities. Cherno nonetheless regards it as highly replicable. Today's engineering students, he says, are more ambitious, more verbal, and less introverted than their predecessors; they tend to embrace the challenge of connecting their chosen profession with larger concerns. For their part, division faculty members value and take seriously the work of helping students in that effort. "Virtually all of us in the division are Ph.D.s in the humanities," Cherno says. "But we think of ourselves as engineering educators."

For more information, contact Melvin Cherno, Joseph L. Vaughan Professor of Humanities and Chair, Division of Humanities, University of Virginia, Charlottesville, Va. 22903.

UNIVERSITY OF FLORIDA

James H. Schaub, distinguished service professor and chairman of the University of Florida's Department of Civil Engineering, is a strong supporter of humanities education for engineers—but not humanities courses as they are traditionally taught to engineers. Traditional humanities courses tend to be well done, he says, and offered by highly qualified faculty members. Because many of these faculty know little about science and engineering, however, obvious and valuable opportunities to relate the humanities to the interests of science and engineering students are overlooked. It is no surprise, says Schaub, that as a result many of these students lose interest in the humanities—or never develop it at all.

This perception, says Schaub, and the belief that there is "a better way to teach humanities to engineers," have led to the creation at Florida of a group of humanities courses that "present the concepts of the humanities disciplines in ways that connect with and appeal to the career interests" of engineering students. Prominent among them is a one-semester course, "Humanities and Engineering," and a two-semester offering, "The History of Technology." Since both courses satisfy university-wide general education requirements, they draw nonengineering students as well. These students are welcomed for the perspectives and stimulation they bring. But these courses also appeal strongly to their target audience; current or prospective engineering majors represent more than half of the enrollments in each.

"Humanities and Engineering" is offered within the College of Engineering, where it is taught by Schaub, who is a civil engineer, and a faculty member from the Classics Department. The syllabus—with major headings such as literature and technology, history and technology, art and technology, and philosophy and engineering—reflects the course's aim to build bridges for prospective engineers from their chosen career field to the concerns of humanistic study. The course is ideally taken early in a student's career so that he or she can choose subsequent H&SS courses having had the introduction to different disciplines that this course provides.

Schaub's "History of Technology" course also reflects his view that liberal education is less a matter of subject matter than approach. Throughout its two semesters—the first treating Europe and the Middle East prior to 1750; the second, Europe and the U.S. from 1740 to World War I—readings and discussions seldom focus on systems and mechanisms per se. Emphasis is on their contexts—the conditions that underlay their development, for example, and the impact they have had on society.

Both "Humanities and Engineering" and "The History of Technology" emphasize the kinds of connections that Schaub says are too often missed in conventional humanities offerings. A discussion of Greek pottery traces the unprecedented beauty of its contrasting black and red colors to chemical processes. The production of these artifacts is discussed as the beginning of the science of ceramics. A study of the culture of Rome emphasizes the central significance of the Roman road system to the development of the empire. In large matters and small, this attention to audience is no less important, says Schaub, than the considerable verve and erudition humanities faculty usually bring to their classes.

Ultimately, however, for all the attention to "bridges" and "contexts" in his courses, Schaub questions the very distinction between technology and the humanities. Technology exists not as an independent system but as an element in the human culture, he argues, paraphrasing Lewis Mumford. In that sense, for Schaub, engineering itself is one of the humanistic disciplines.

In several respects the Florida courses are typical of like offerings at other institutions. First, they were developed with grant support—in this case a grant in 1975 from the National Endowment for the Humanities that underwrote a considerable amount of interdisiciplinary course development and team teaching designed to integrate humanistic and professional preparation in business, pre-law, and pre-medicine, as well as engineering. They are typical also in that they have known hard times. As funding has diminished, departments have had less financial incentive to assign faculty to these courses. And this particular kind of interdisciplinary work has not proved likely to strengthen a case for tenure or promotion. Finally—and in this, too, the Florida courses seem representative of at least some others elsewhere—they thrive today largely as labors of love on the part of faculty who have insisted on teaching them. Faculty initiative and leadership are simply essential to the success of such offerings. As Schaub points out, "these courses can't be assigned."

For more information, contact James H. Schaub, Professor and Chair, Department of Civil Engineering, University of Florida, Gainesville, Fla. 32611.

HARVEY MUDD COLLEGE

California's Harvey Mudd College is known for providing engineering students a strong education in the humanities and social sciences. Not only is every engineering major's H&SS coursework planned out with care, but it consists of no fewer than twelve courses taken over four years—representing, in effect, a minor in the liberal arts.

This emphasis on liberal studies is not new to Harvey Mudd, a small (enrollment approximately 550), highly selective member of the Claremont Colleges group. Harvey Mudd graduates only engineering and science majors. But the idea was central to its founding in 1955 that, in order to be equipped for leadership in their professions and society, Harvey Mudd graduates should have to grapple at a significant level with the humanities and social sciences. In fact, the current requirement of twelve H&SS courses is itself a relaxation of an original requirement of fourteen. By and large, however, the original array of requirements developed to ensure depth, breadth, and coherence of H&SS coursework is still in place today. Also well established is a twelve-member department of the humanities and social sciences, representing just under one-fifth of the entire Harvey Mudd faculty.

The Harvey Mudd H&SS requirement consists of two broad parts: two one-semester freshman courses—Rhetoric and Humanities II—and ten elective courses taken over the next three years. Rhetoric is a literature-based writing course emphasizing reading and argumentative thought. Humanities II is an introduction to college-level research and discussion skills in the humanities and social sciences. It is offered in six to eight optional sections with different, often thematic and interdisciplinary, emphases. Integrative in approach, these freshman-year courses provide an important foundation for further study. It is, however, the shape and extent of the additional ten-course H&SS requirement that sets apart Harvey Mudd's approach.

A rigorous four-part requirement governs the choice of the ten H&SS electives:

☐ As a general distribution requirement, the undergraduate engineer must take at least one course in each of the following areas: history, literature, philosophy, pyschology, and social and political institutions.

☐ He or she must concentrate in one area, taking four courses that together explore that subject in some depth. Imaginative arrangements are actively encouraged; for example, a Japanese culture concentration might combine appropriate coursework in history, economics, language, and art.

☐ He or she must take at least five courses of the ten from the Harvey Mudd Humanities and Social Sciences Department. The other five may be taken in any of the other institutions within the Claremont Colleges, which collectively offer a wide selection of humanities and social sciences courses.

☐ One course of the ten must be a "senior seminar," a research project supervised on a tutorial basis by one of the H&SS faculty.

These policies and requirements are designed to foster an extensive, carefully conceived, and closely supervised experience in the humanities and social sciences marked by both breadth and depth of study; taken together, they provide incentive to explore, freedom to choose, and opportunity to pursue subjects of individual interest at an advanced level.

One key to the effectiveness of the ten-course requirement is that each engineering student has, in addition to a major advisor, a designated H&SS advisor from the Humanities and Social Sciences Department faculty. The H&SS advisor works individually with the student to ensure that his or her choice of courses conforms to the four-part requirement and otherwise adds up to a coherent academic experience.

Although a quarter to a third of Harvey Mudd's H&SS courses make important reference to technology and the sciences, according to Professor Tad Beckman, the department's chair, they are not as a rule tailored to engineers. Some offerings are interdisiplinary, but most tend to be "field-specific" and to reflect the academic backgrounds of the faculty who teach them (in three cases, literature; in two cases each, philosophy, history, psychology, and government; and in one case, economics). Rather than providing engineering students "bridges" from their own field of study, in short, Harvey Mudd faculty more often expect their students to encounter the humanities and social sciences entirely on those disciplines' own terms.

H&SS requirements like Harvey Mudd's naturally exert pressure elsewhere on the curriculum, especially since the college requires the student to take an extensive "technical core" of mathematics and science in addition to engineering courses. The college's general engineering program may even now be the minimum in extent that can be accredited. The college's own science and engineering faculty nonetheless are said to respect and support the emphasis on the humanities and social sciences, and understand its centrality to the institution's mission. So, tellingly, do its alumni/ae. Although studies show that younger graduates tend to wish they had had more specialized coursework, Beckman reports, those who have been out six years or more tend to look back on their H&SS experience as a particularly important—and professionally valuable—part of their college education.

For more information, contact Tad Beckman, Professor and Chair, Department of Humanities and Social Sciences, Harvey Mudd College, Claremont, Calif. 91711.

WORCESTER POLYTECHNIC INSTITUTE

Worcester Polytechnic Institute figures prominently in most conversations on innovative engineering curricula. A college of science and engineering in Worcester, Massachusetts, enrolling approximately thirty-eight hundred students (including twenty-six hundred undergraduates), WPI boldly recast its entire undergraduate program in the spring of 1970. It eliminated required courses and established performance-based requirements for graduation. Although the original open curriculum is now more constrained, other key components of the "WPI Plan" are in place and thriving. These include two that are of particular interest here: the requirements that students complete both a "humanities sufficiency" and an "interactive qualifying project."

One of the chief architects of the "WPI Plan," Dean of Undergraduate Studies William R. Grogan, explains the problem these requirements were designed some twenty years ago to address: "We recognized that while our courses were good at information transfer, they didn't attend well to personal development, to communications skills, to cultural understanding. They were effective at teaching analysis but not at teaching synthesis—pulling together ideas to solve large comprehensive problems. In addition, we were too cloistered here on campus. We didn't give our students nearly enough awareness of the strong two-way relationship between technology and society."

Grogan, then a professor of electrical engineering, and his colleagues saw in these problems a strong case for increased emphasis on the liberal arts, which at that time students and faculty members "didn't take very seriously." The reforms that they successfully championed have encouraged more—and more coherent—study in the humanities per se and the integration of humanistic and social perspectives into substantial portions of students' engineering coursework.

The humanities sufficiency is a requirement that each student complete five or more thematically related courses in the humanities; these courses must also be followed by an independent research activity (usually a critical or research essay, but sometimes a performance or work of art, instead) that synthesizes and extends the student's work through a mini-thesis. This requirement essentially ensures that every WPI graduate completes the equivalent of a minor in the humanities—but a minor that because of its thematic focus allows more study in depth than most. "Basically," says Grogan, "there are two schools of thought about humanities and the engineer. One holds that a student should get a little bit of everything, which means required survey courses. The second argument, the one we ultimately embraced, says that it is better to master one area than to get a superficial sprinkling of many." Some might find this characterization of the available options restrictive, but few would argue with WPI's rationale for its choice. Given other claims on the undergraduate engineer's academic attentions, planting seeds of an interest in the humanities that might be pursued later must be one of the goals of undergraduate classwork. A policy of encouraging students to use their limited time for study in some depth—really to learn, as the catalogue puts it, "how knowledge is obtained and expressed in a nontechnical discipline"—may be the best assurance of their developing a "sufficient" understanding of an area of the humanities to engender such a lifelong interest.

Each student's sufficiency is planned in consultation with an advisor from WPI's humanities faculty. So long as it is thematically related, sufficiency coursework may be entirely in one discipline or it may involve several disciplines. In any case, it typically extends from the freshman through the junior years.

WPI's humanities sufficiency is an unusual engineering requirement, but the requirement of an Interactive Qualifying Project (IQP) is probably unique. The IQP is a substantial project completed during the junior year and equivalent in time to at least three conventional courses. Although students have great freedom in choosing their projects, their topics must have both a significant technical component and an important humanistic and/or societal dimension. The very purpose of the IQP is to "introduce students to the priorities and concerns of nontechnical elements of society"—in other words, those nonscientists and nonengineers who constitute most of society, including much of its leadership. By "interacting," ideally, with selected laypersons, as well as by doing more conventional research, the engineering student doing an IQP learns firsthand something of the challenge of "relating . . . science or technology to social needs and social issues."

WPI attaches such importance to the IQP that it has established what Grogan calls "an enormous support system" for it. An entirely new academic division, the Division of Interdisciplinary Affairs, has been created and staffed by faculty members whose principal appointments are in other areas. Coordinated by faculty members who receive additional compensation for their work, some eleven subdivisions organize and facilitate project activity in such areas as technology and environment, risk analysis and liability, health care and technology, humanistic studies of technology, and social and human services. The subdivisions help interested students find appropriate preparatory coursework. This last usually includes the two social science courses required of all WPI students entirely apart from the humanities sufficiency and the IQP.

WPI also has restructured its calendar to support its system of requirements, under which one-third of a student's academic life in the upper years is devoted to independent projects. A Major Qualifying Project (MQP) of similar dimensions also is required in the senior year. Seven-week terms, in which students take only three courses at a time, enable them to give their IQPs substantial attention and to undertake projects in small groups if they wish. These shorter terms also facilitate off-campus fieldwork, a common component of the IQP, and student use of any of several "project centers."

These project centers are programs through which faculty commit a portion of their teaching and research activity to an ongoing topic that generates new IQP projects annually. A project center established in Washington, D.C., in 1973 has now supported nearly six hundred IQPs. A London center has recently been opened, and a number of others—on topics as various as juvenile delinquency, museums, municipal studies, and solar electrification—operate on or near the WPI campus.

A selection of titles can only suggest the diversity of IQP topics: "The Greenhouse Effect"; "Sex Discrimination in Scientific Imagery"; "Employment Impact of Robotics"; "Behavioral Approaches to Design"; "One-kilowatt Power Supply for Tanzania"; and "Stress Levels at WPI."

One-third of WPI's living alumni have now graduated under the program that requires the sufficiency and the IQP, and their support of it, Grogan says, is "almost universally very, very strong." They connect it with a special readiness on their parts to deal with the nontechnical dimensions of problems, a quality they regard as of great value professionally and otherwise. "The major qualifying project got me my job," one alumnus has commented. "The IQP has changed my life."

Is the program replicable elsewhere? Grogan says that components clearly are. The sufficiency, for one, has had a number of adaptations. The IQP, he believes, may be a function of a special time in the 1970s when engineering and science faculties were especially willing to consider and contribute to fundamental curricular reform. And he points out that the IQP is still somewhat difficult to sustain, since new faculty members often need to be "socialized" to it, their resistance and skepticism overcome. The good news, he says, is that "most faculty come to value the requirement. I ask them to participate in one or two projects a year in an area that means something to them." With some fourteen hundred MQPs and IQPs underway at any one time, faculty involvement and the program itself remain strong.

UNFINISHED DESIGN

For more information, contact William R. Grogan, Dean of Undergraduate Studies, Worcester Polytechnic Institute, 100 Institute Road, Worcester, Mass. 01609.

CALIFORNIA STATE POLYTECHNIC UNIVERSITY–POMONA

Students intending to major in engineering at California State Polytechnic University–Pomona can choose an unusual alternative to the humanities and social science component of their institution's established general education curriculum. Designed expressly for students in the schools of agriculture, architecture, business administration, engineering, environmental design, and science, Cal Poly's Interdisciplinary General Education (IGE) Program is a structured sequence of eight quarter-long courses taken over two-and-a-half years. It was developed in the early 1980s with the strong support of the deans of those schools in response to what was then a general dissatisfaction with the fragmentation and ineffectiveness of the traditional general education curriculum. Today these professional schools remain the program's only source of students. Of the two hundred freshmen enrolling in the program each year, 75 to 80 percent are prospective engineers; in all, some 10 to 15 percent of Cal Poly's engineering majors pursue their general education through this program.

The founders of the IGE program believe courses traditionally offered as general education too often stress the knowledge requisite to humanities and social science majors rather than their students' broad cognitive development. They see their program, by contrast, as giving professional, technically oriented students an experience in the humanities that deals in an open-ended way with the central issues of the human condition. Each of the program's courses seeks to develop cross-cultural literacy, a grasp of the moral and ethical implications of knowledge (especially scientific and technical knowledge), critical-thinking and problem-solving skills, and a critical appreciation of artistic forms of expression.

IGE courses are offered in a loose chronological order. The three first-year courses move from the origins of human society, through the ancient world, to the Renaissance. Second-year courses cover the expansion of the West, the Enlightenment, and the Industrial Age. The modern world is the focus of the first of the two third-year courses, the second of which is a capstone seminar. The purpose of this "loose historical grid" is not, however, an accumulation of historical information, emphasizes Richard C. Jacobs, the program conductor. It is "to provide a context for ideas—always the program's target." Accordingly, a sequence of major themes is explored through the program's historical lens: rationalism and revelations in connection with the ancient world, for example, and individualism and collectivism in the context of the Industrial Revolution. Although appropriate reference is made to technology, emphasis in this program is on "the wisdom and knowledge base of the humanities."

A number of elements contribute to the richness and uniqueness of the IGE program, including Jacob's strong interest in educational experimentation. All courses are team taught, and faculty are drawn from approximately a dozen disciplines. They meet extensively, without released time or compensation, to plan and coordinate their offerings, and they consciously employ a variety of meeting formats, activities, and interactive pedagogical approaches. A primary goal, says Jacobs, is a sense of shared enquiry, of participation in a "democratic learning community."

As such vocabulary suggests, the program exemplifies a spirit of educational reform in some respects more typical of the 1960s than the present. Whatever its wellsprings, the IGE Program seems to draw strength from them. Recognized already at the campus, system, and national levels, it promises to be a source of continuing innovation.

For more information, contact Richard C. Jacobs, Coordinator, Interdisciplinary General Education Program, California State Polytechnic University–Pomona, 3801 West Temple Avenue, Pomona, Calif. 91768-4050.

UNIVERSITY OF ILLINOIS AT URBANA-CHAMPAIGN

The College of Engineering at the University of Illinois at Urbana-Champaign (UIUC) has an array of popular and cost-effective programs providing engineering undergraduates limited opportunities for international study. But this was not always so.

The problem, as Associate Dean Howard Wakeland explains, was the difficulty of using the traditional exchange and foreign-study programs serving students in the arts and sciences. These proved largely impractical for most engineers, requiring more time abroad and more formal language study than the engineering curriculum usually allows.

Then some fifteen years ago, UIUC began an involvement with the International Association for the Exchange of Students for Technical Experience (IAESTE), an independent organization that offers an alternative to traditional arrangements. IAESTE provides technically trained students here and abroad opportunities to gain work experience in other countries, typically for a period of a few months, often during the summer. To date, 350 UIUC engineering students have held technical traineeships through IAESTE. They have taken placements in all parts of Europe as well as in Turkey, Israel, Thailand, Japan, Korea, and South America. Some fifteen to twenty more do so each year.

It was, however, the subsequent establishment of an endowed fund to support student travel that really got the College of Engineering's international efforts off the ground. With original funding from alumnus Armand Elmendorf and additional support more recently from private industry, the Elmendorf Travel Award assists all undergraduate engineers in their travel as they undertake foreign schooling or educationally related work experiences. "It's remarkable," says Wakeland, "how diverse our students are and how much they already are doing or want to be doing internationally on their own. With these travel awards we can bring the cost within the realm of possibility. This way," he adds, "we also are aware of their involvements." Last year fifty-two UIUC engineering students were provided partial travel grants ranging from $250 for a trip to the United Kingdom to $1,000 for travel to Japan. Wakeland admits to favoring requests involving travel to non-English speaking countries. Whatever their destinations, recipients enroll in a one semester-hour course and provide a report after completing their study.

In recent years, even as exchanges and travel grants have sparked the interest of engineering students in international experiences, the UIUC engineering faculty noticed that entering students are better prepared to take advantage of them. In particular, students are enrolling with more high school language study. Last year, in fact, 50 percent of entering freshmen had a full three years or more—and 90 percent, two or more years—even though foreign language is not a UIUC requirement. In this trend UIUC has found an opportunity to do more with language study for engineers than had been previously attempted. Whereas in the past, UIUC, like most engineering schools, had ignored students' language training and essentially had encouraged them to turn their attention to other things, Wakeland has begun writing to all entering freshmen encouraging them to continue studying in college the language they have studied in high school. The initial results have been encouraging. Many more students are beginning college language study at intermediate levels. Engineering enrollments in courses in one language, German, have increased fourfold.

Students who commit to studying a language at the college level have a high continuation rate; most take at least two years at the college level and many take three or four. Especially when combined with prior study, this persistence in language study makes it possible even for many engineering students to reach a point of some fluency. In this case, as with the travel award, Wakeland suggests, UIUC's success has been largely a matter of recognizing and building upon the strengths and interests students themselves are presenting.

This strategy of building directly on high school coursework works less well in the case of a number of languages with which tomorrow's engineers may most need to be familiar—for example, Korean, Japanese, Chinese, and Russian. None of these languages accounts for more than one-tenth of one percent of U.S. high school language instruction. Thus, although a growing number of Asian-Americans bring some language background that they can be encouraged to develop, most native English speakers interested in these languages must start with introductory courses at the college level. That, nonetheless, is something Wakeland encourages interested engineering students to do, just as he encourages interested students to begin one of the romance languages even if they have no background in it. Wakeland considers some limited oral capability a worthwhile and achievable goal in these cases.

The UIUC College of Engineering recently created a formal international studies minor that combines travel and language study with culturally related coursework. The minor, which may be concentrated in such areas as Chinese, Asian, or European studies, requires a work or study experience of eight weeks or longer in the appropriate region, twelve semester hours in related cultural studies, and one advanced course in comparative economics or political science. It also requires language proficiency at the second-year college level—a level, again, that many entering engineering students can now attain in less than two full years. The college's experience suggests that the requirements of the minor can be met, in many cases, by using the half-year of coursework required by all engineering programs in the humanities and social sciences and the additional six or more hours available to UIUC engineers in free electives. The program is popular and growing rapidly.

An imaginative *quid pro quo* arrangement drives another initiative, the new "targeted area program," begun in 1986. The program began with the observation, says Wakeland, that like many U.S. engineering schools, UIUC routinely "gives away" something highly prized in other countries: the opportunity to pursue graduate training in engineering in the U.S. If UIUC were to insist on certain things in return from foreign institutions sending UIUC their students for graduate study, Wakeland and his colleagues reasoned, UIUC's American students' international opportunities might be still further expanded.

The arrangements struck with two Chinese institutions in Nanjing and Wuhan reflect the eventual rate of exchange. UIUC "traded" one half-time U.S. graduate assistantship worth $6,500 and a waiver of out-of-state tuition worth $5,600 in exchange for agreement from each Chinese institution to:
☐ send its top engineering student to Illinois to take the assistantship and
☐ accept five UIUC engineering undergraduates for an eight-week summer period, furnish them room and board, and arrange for them both a six-week on-site program (entailing a half-day of instruction in oral Chinese and a half-day of work in business or industry) and a two-week tour of the country.

This first exchange with China was quite successful. Wakeland reports that it greatly increased the U.S. participants' understanding of Chinese culture and society. Although their only Chinese prior to their three weeks in the country was an intensive five semester-hour course, Wakeland also claims that they reached a level of limited proficiency in the spoken language by the time of their return.

This barter-like form of exchange, which trades highly sought U.S. resources for services desired from abroad, currently figures in UIUC arrangements with several institutions in South America. In the future, the College of Engineering hopes to initiate similar exchanges with Korea, Japan, and the Soviet Union.

Elements of the UIUC program will strike those accustomed to traditional language training and foreign study in the arts and sciences as superficial. For his part Wakeland admits that this array of international programs and arrangements at UIUC's College of Engineering provides most students, at best, basic language-level skills and understandings. "We're not producing experts. We are providing a foundation students can build on with further travel and study—with the full understanding that the rest is up to them." Given other current constraints on the engineer's time, that goal, he implies, may be the most ambitious one that can be attained.

For more information, contact Howard L. Wakeland, Associate Dean, College of Engineering, 207 Engineering Hall, 1308 West Green Street, University of Illinois at Urbana-Champaign, Urbana, Ill. 61801.

INNOVATIVE PROGRAMS

UNIVERSITY OF ROCHESTER

Two years ago the University of Rochester announced an extraordinary policy. A number of interested students whose majors afford them little elective freedom but who have strong and coherent plans of study in the liberal arts would be allowed to extend their undergraduate work by an additional semester or year, and the university would forgive their tuitions for the additional period of enrollment.

The new policy, dubbed "Take Five," was designed in part as an answer to the unusually imposing set of requirements governing engineering coursework. University officials believed that if given the chance, many engineering majors in particular would take better advantage of the institution's resources in the arts and sciences. As long as the number of students participating at any time were limited, these officials reasoned, they could be added to existing courses at little marginal cost to the university.

The first two years of the program's operation have borne out these assumptions. The program has proven popular, with three students applying for every available spot. Although participants have included students majoring in a variety of the arts and sciences, thirty of the forty students admitted so far have been engineers. Moreover, despite a general undergraduate tuition of $11,000, the university is carrying the program on its own budget. The only outside funding has been a grant from the Fund for the Improvement of Postsecondary Education to support the advising, career counseling, and academic monitoring of the participants.

Applicants apply when they declare an academic concentration—generally in their sophomore or junior years—with a plan outlining both a four-year and an extended course of study and an essay spelling out their educational goals. These materials are reviewed by a committee of faculty members, administrators, and students, which looks for both depth and coherence in the proposed coursework. Applicants may propose to develop second majors or minors. However, the additional coursework, which is typically spread over the junior, senior, and fifth years, cannot be in the student's primary major and cannot be vocational in character.

Participation in the "Take-Five" program is not without cost, as students must pay room and board and forego a semester or a year's wages. Some 10 percent of Rochester's undergraduate engineers choose the option, nonetheless—evidence that at least in their judgments such costs are outweighed by the benefits of a somewhat broader education.

For more information, contact Ruth Freeman, University Dean and Associate Provost, Office of the Provost, 200 Administration, University of Rochester, Rochester, N.Y. 14627.

COLORADO SCHOOL OF MINES

To those who do not know the institution, the Colorado School of Mines might seem an unlikely setting for an interdisciplinary honors program in public affairs. CSM graduates only engineering majors—and in energy-related fields of engineering at that. In 1979, however, a small group of like-minded CSM faculty members from engineering and liberal arts set out to create such a program on their Golden, Colorado, campus. It was important, they felt, for at least some of their most talented and motivated students, "to have an educational experience of excellence in the liberal arts." Their rationale—that active liberal learning has a special role to play in preparing flexible, broadly gauged managers and leaders for the twenty-first century—was not uncommon. Their persistence and good fortune was.

Having been launched successfully with support from the National Endowment for the Humanities, then renamed and endowed in honor of a retired CSM president, The Guy T. McBride, Jr., Honors Program in Public Affairs for Engineers is today a thriving "college within a college," an educational experiment that enjoys widespread campus support. Between 35 and 40 of CSM's 350 freshmen are admitted to the McBride Honors Program each year. They are selected on the basis not only of high school and first-semester college grades, but their test scores, extracurricular activities (including foreign travel and their participation in arts), an interview, recommendations from their instructors, and a personal essay.

A student's work in the program begins in the spring semester of the freshman year and continues through the fall semester of the senior year. He or she takes a semester-long interdisciplinary seminar each term for five terms, then undertakes an internship or overseas study and travel in the summer following the junior year. A capstone senior course completes the program in the first semester of the senior year. All told, completion of the program requires twenty-one semester hours, fulfills much of CSM's

H&SS requirement, and qualifies the student for a minor in public affairs.

Each of the five central seminars, according to program literature, serves the overall program goal of helping students "understand the increasing complexity of their future professional environment, national and global, and assume management and leadership responsibilities in the years ahead." After the first seminar, "Western Intellectual and Cultural Heritage," students take another in area studies, choosing sections focusing on either the U.S. or the Third World. Both area studies offerings emphasize the role of technology in development and its impact on social change.

In their junior year all students take a fall seminar in international relations, and then choose between two spring offerings. One is a seminar in public policy. The other, a prerequisite for students interested in overseas study the following summer, is a class in an appropriate foreign language. After the summer internship/overseas program, students converge for the final capstone course. During this, their last semester in the sequence, teams of two students each work on an engineering design or public policy project of their choice in the context of all they have learned in the program.

According to program brochures, the McBride Program seeks to inspire "a sense of intellectual community, love of learning, and active student engagement in the learning process." Toward that end, participating faculty, called "tutors," do not lecture but "moderate"; students initiate and carry discussion. The frequent use of presentations, debates, literature-based improvisations, and the like helps break down students' inhibitions, and collegial one-on-one tutorials with moderators have an important place in every seminar.

Perhaps the feature that most sets the program apart is that every session of each seminar, with its enrollment of fifteen to twenty students, is staffed by three faculty members. One of these, designated the "principal moderator," is generally a humanist or a social scientist. The other two, "associate moderators," are always professors in science and engineering. Most associate moderators are senior faculty members who are not compensated for their participation and have been provided no released time for it. Nonetheless, they help design the seminar, complete all the assigned readings, take part in all discussions, and participate in the evaluation of students. In addition to helping ensure that different disciplinary perspectives are brought into the course, the active involvement of these scientists and engineers gives the program credibility in students' eyes. It is a sign of the program's growing faculty support that more engineering and science faculty than can be accommodated

UNFINISHED DESIGN

now want to serve as tutors.

Asked how much the seminars are tailored specifically to engineers, Philipose speaks of "a judicious selection of liberal arts approaches and themes that come closest to the engineering profession." A discussion of fine arts, he explains, may focus on sculpture, an art form sometimes more accessible than others to engineers. A study of *King Lear* is less likely to center on the play's language than on its commentary on the abuses of power. And the international relations seminar emphasizes technology transfer. "Too few in the liberal arts realize that the future of these subjects depends largely on how they are taught in professional schools," says Philipose, "and that with professional students the approaches usually used to teach liberal arts majors tend to be ineffective."

Despite the program's relative newness, Philipose and his colleagues have evidence of its effectiveness. Companies actively recruit interns and graduates from the program, and the Colorado Commission for Higher Education has conferred on it a $50,000 Recognition of Excellence Award. But there is still more encouraging evidence, says Philipose. Graduates are enrolling in graduate schools at a rate higher than that of CSM graduates overall and are competing for and winning national awards and fellowships that have traditionally been the province of liberal arts students. There is a "positive osmosis effect" on students who are not in the McBride Program, says Philipose. "Our program sends a message."

For more information, contact Thomas Philipose, Principal Tutor, Guy T. McBride, Jr., Honors Program in Public Affairs for Engineers, Colorado School of Mines, Golden, Colo. 80401.

MASSACHUSETTS INSTITUTE OF TECHNOLOGY

Signs of major change at the Massachusetts Institute of Technology, a leading school of engineering, tend to attract widespread attention. Such was the case in late spring of 1987 when—after vigorous debate and student opposition—MIT's faculty approved a set of proposals intended to broaden the education of engineering undergraduates.

The vote was the first outcome of what has been, to date, a three-year review of the undergraduate program. Over that period, three faculty committees—including MIT's Committee on the Humanities, Arts and Social Sciences (HASS) Requirements—had agreed to a call for sweeping curricular change. Current arrangements, the consensus had it, produced engineers too narrowly focused either for their personal or professional well-being or for the good of society. Although requirements called for students to take at least eight courses outside of the sciences, mathematics, and engineering—including three from a list of 156 approved options and three others in one area (for example, psychology or history)—they did not ensure sufficiently structured study. Of particular concern was the wide range of optional offerings, many of them low-level survey courses, that did not seem to be serving any overall concept of general education.

With its spring 1987 vote, the faculty approved two fundamental modifications that affect all undergraduates entering MIT in the fall of 1988 and thereafter. First the faculty left the HASS core requirement unchanged in terms of classroom hours and credits but reduced the number and increased the coherence of the options by which students can fulfill the distribution portion of the requirement. Students now will select one course in each of at least three of five new thematic categories: Literary and Textual Studies; Language, Thought and Value; the Arts; Cultures and Societies; and Historical Studies. Courses in these categories will reflect appropriately the full range of contemporary scholarship, including that on women, minorities, and non-Western cultures, and include work in language acquisition and the visual arts. As before, at least one of these three required courses will be in the humanities and at least one in the social sciences.

The second change was approval of a new "minor" program that, for the first time, will provide undergraduates the formal option of in-depth work in an augmented HASS area. The current requirement of three related courses in one nontechnical academic area remains unchanged, but students may now take a total of six with a specific area of concentration. According to MIT's *Technology Review*,[23] "The tiered nature of groups of subjects approved as minors" will ensure academic experiences in HASS areas "much more demanding and penetrating" than any most undergraduates now have.

These reforms, emphasizes Margaret L. MacVicar, dean for undergraduate education, are only the beginning of an effort to bring about a more integrated educational experience for MIT students. MIT faculty have committed themselves to developing new courses, especially interdisciplinary ones taught jointly by faculty members from both "the humanistic disciplines and the technical ones," explains MacVicar. Consideration is even being given to requiring some courses in addition to the HASS requirement—a move that

MIT officials think would force the issue of whether a four-year period of study is adequate for the preparation of engineers.

According to MIT President Paul E. Gray, MIT is "not considering just a fine-tuning of the curriculum, but a recasting of the educational mission."[24] Whatever the course of events, then, further changes seem likely. It seems clear, moreover, that MIT will give new prominence to the role of the humanities, arts, and social sciences in preparing some of the nation's most able engineers.

For more information, contact Margaret L. MacVicar, Dean for Undergraduate Education, Massachusetts Institute of Technology, 77 Massachusetts Avenue, Cambridge, Mass. 02139.

DARTMOUTH COLLEGE

Just after the Civil War, when General Sylvanus Thayer wanted to endow a graduate school of engineering, he purposefully sought out a liberal arts college to be the recipient of his generosity. Thayer, who as superintendent from 1817 to 1833 had established the U.S. Military Academy as the nation's first engineering school, had strong convictions about how one becomes an engineer. Before embarking on a professional course of study, one should first become "a gentleman"— that is, study the liberal arts. Only then, and at the graduate level, should one specialize in engineering.[25]

Thayer chose New Hampshire's Dartmouth College, a strong liberal arts institution, as the home of what was to become the Thayer School of Engineering. In 1867, he gave the college $40,000 to establish a two-year graduate program for students who had completed a full four-year undergraduate education. By 1893, Dartmouth had devised a way of combining a student's undergraduate and professional coursework—an arrangement that produced a five-year program.[26] From time to time in the years since, other institutions, frustrated by the difficulty of providing both a broad and a technical education within four years, have experimented with similar designs. But almost all have reverted, under the pressure of economic competition, to the four-year format. Dartmouth's program, however, has survived and thrived. Whether it is a vestige of the past or a harbinger of the future is an issue engineering educators debate.

For all the singularity of Dartmouth's program, the issue of whether other institutions should adopt the five-year model seems very

INNOVATIVE
PROGRAMS

much alive. The issues are complex and have as much to do with cost and the time required for technical education as they do with engineers' need for breadth in the humanities and social sciences. Nonetheless—whatever its other strengths or weaknesses—the five-year program allows more time for the production of liberally educated engineers, so a brief account of how it works at Dartmouth is in order.

High school students interested in studying engineering at Dartmouth apply through the same admissions process as all other Dartmouth applicants, and if they are accepted, they enroll, like their peers, in the college. There, they take a regular four-year program, meeting the same distribution requirements in the humanities, social sciences, natural sciences, and foreign languages as other Dartmouth undergraduates. They also complete additional science and math courses and an eight-course major in engineering sciences—the latter offered by faculty holding dual appointments in the College of Arts and Sciences and in the graduate engineering school. They graduate in four years with a bachelor of arts (A.B.) degree with a major in engineering sciences. Although this four-year program is not accredited, it provides what the college describes as "the broadest possible interdisciplinary engineering education." Many students—40 percent in recent years—take no further work in engineering; in many cases, these students enter professional schools of law or medicine. But 60 percent or so of Dartmouth's engineering sciences graduates typically continue at the Thayer School, taking only graduate engineering courses for an additional two or three quarters. With this additonal coursework they can complete an accredited bachelor of engineering (B.E.) degree program.

Students who decide on an engineering major as late as the end of their sophomore year can still complete the Dartmouth program within five years. Those, on the other hand, who decide early and choose to take their free electives in engineering can finish in thirteen or, in a few cases, even twelve quarters. To do this, however, runs counter, in a sense, to the program's liberalizing intentions. And since Dartmouth operates on a year-round calendar, additional terms of study can usually be planned to ensure a minimum of inconvenience.

Thayer School officials readily admit that although their graduates are in great demand, the expense of the additional terms of study is considerable, and thus a problem. They maintain, however, that the real question may be what one gets for one's money. Their answer, at least, is "the total engineer"—both broadly educated and technically proficient.

For more information, contact Horst J.

UNFINISHED DESIGN

Richter, Professor of Engineering and Director of Undergraduate Studies, Thayer School of Engineering, Dartmouth College, Hanover, N.H. 03755.

CALVIN COLLEGE

Calvin College, in Grand Rapids, Michigan, takes seriously its mission as an institution of the Christian Reformed Church. Accordingly, says Department of Engineering Chair Lambert J. Van Poolen, its engineering program not only teaches "straight engineering" but also presents technology as "an integral part of a unified creation" and "a resource to be used in service." Few other engineering programs are apt ever to characterize their missions in such terms. Some may take inspiration, however, from the distinctive combination of approaches used by Calvin's engineering department to translate the college's ideals into educational practice. H&SS-related coursework in Calvin's engineering curriculum includes a core of nine liberal arts courses and a team-taught interdisciplinary January interim course in technology and the humanities. In addition, far more than at most institutions, professional engineering courses are themselves designed as vehicles for liberal learning.

The nine conventional liberal arts courses taken by engineering majors include two in literature; four in other fields of the humanities (of which two must be in philosophy and one in religion); two in the social sciences (of which one must be in economics); and one in the fine arts or foreign culture. This core, which is nearly as broad and as extensive as that required of nonengineers at Calvin, is taught entirely by liberal arts faculty and makes no special reference to technology.

By contrast, the technology and humanities course taken by junior majors during their January interim is explicitly interdisciplinary. Students have a choice of three sections, each taught by two or more faculty, one of whom is always an engineer. One option in 1987 was "Philosophy of Technology," which was taught by a philosopher and an engineer. The course is designed to build on its students' prior work in philosophy to develop a relatively advanced understanding of technology and its impacts and to examine some of the most significant critiques and defenses of technology from a philosophical and religious perspective. A second option for the interim, "Computer and Culture," had similar goals but was team taught by four faculty: an engineer, an economist, a philosopher, and

INNOVATIVE
PROGRAMS

an artist.

By far the most unusual interim option was the third which, according to the Calvin catalogue, took students into Appalachian Kentucky "to describe, analyze, and resolve a large-scale, real-world, socio-technical problem: that of creating sustainable employment in an economically underdeveloped area." The class—nine engineers and seven students from other disciplines—first spent a week in preparatory work on campus, organizing themselves into two teams, electing project managers, researching the problems and conditions of life in eastern Kentucky, hearing speakers familiar with the region, and developing ideas for economic development projects. They then spent ten days in Kentucky, meeting residents, observing their way of life, and interviewing members of social agencies and other organizations at work in the area. While in Kentucky, the Calvin students also made presentations on their ideas for businesses that could be established and taken over by area residents. In a final week back on campus, students chose their best ideas and wrote their project reports. The final recommendation of this year's class: using the vacated limestone caves so common in eastern Kentucky for mushroom farming. Next year's recommendation promises to be different; the class will be looking for ways to improve the economic life of inner-city Grand Rapids.

Marvin Vander Wal, the engineering professor who co-taught the 1987 Appalachian course, describes Calvin's as a particularly rich form of experiential education. It provides students experiences with communication, group dynamics, and decision making, and first-hand exposure to people and places and social problems of types most have not encountered previously. It drives home a central theme of all of Calvin's H&SS related courses: that great sensitivity to context and much careful research are required for a successful design, one that works not only mechanically, but psychologically, culturally, ethically, politically, and philosophically. Even the sustained interaction with students majoring in fields other than engineering is beneficial, says Vander Wal. It forces engineers to broaden their perspectives and look at more aspects of a problem than they otherwise would.

Calvin's effort to enforce attention to engineering's broader contexts and to encourage a philosophical perspective on its content pervades the engineering curriculum. Indeed, Van Poolen maintains that when he and his colleagues are doing their job they "don't offer any ordinary engineering courses." Certainly syllabi for both the freshman and senior design courses make it clear that while the requisite technical material is well covered, topics such as aesthetics, the socioeconomic evaluation of projects, and the role of values and ethics in design also get prominent consideration. Even what might seem the most unlikely course in this regard provides the philosophically minded Van Poolen, an engineer, opportunities to encourage open-ended modes of inquiry: "For instance, I like to caution my students in 'Heat Transfer' that everything in the textbook is historically conditioned by the problems people have had to solve," he says. "They need to be aware how big the gaps can be between reality and how we model it."

For more information, contact Lambert J. Van Poolen, Professor and Chair, Department of Engineering, Calvin College, Grand Rapids, Mich. 49506.

STANFORD UNIVERSITY

A number of studies have called attention in recent years to college students' ignorance of the Western tradition. The undergraduates at Stanford's School of Engineering, however, tend to be relatively well acquainted with that tradition. They not only fulfill university-wide distribution requirements, they also join their peers in a mandatory, three-quarter course sequence in some broad aspect of Western culture.

There are seven "tracks" or course sequences within this Western/Culture core, each treating major works and historical movements:

- "Great Works of Western Culture"
- "Europe: From the Middle Ages to the Present"
- "Western Thought and Literature"
- "Ideas in Western Culture"
- "Western Culture and Technology"
- "Conflict and Change in Western Culture," and
- "Literature and the Arts in Western Culture."

The "Western Culture and Technology" sequence, taught within the university's Values, Technology, and Society program, is especially popular among prospective engineers. Engineering students' enrollment in this track, however, is carefully limited.

The syllabi of the seven tracks are all built on a common master list of major texts. It includes required readings in Genesis, Plato, Homer, Greek tragedy, the New Testament, Augustine, Dante, More, Machiavelli, Luther, Galileo, Voltaire, Marx, Engels, Freud, and Darwin. Another list of readings is "strongly recommended" for all tracks. Each track also adds readings appropriate to its particular focus. The student's commitment of time and effort to his or her Western Culture course is substantial. It carries five units of credit, reflecting in most cases three one-hour lectures weekly by senior faculty and a weekly two-hour small discussion, led by a graduate or postdoctoral student.

In addition to the Western Culture requirement, engineers complete at least one course in each of four distribution areas: literature and fine arts; philosophical, social, and religious thought; human development, behavior, and language; and social processes and institutions. They also fulfill requirements (which some waive by examination) of two and three quarters, respectively, in English and a foreign language.

The result of curricular reform seven years ago, Stanford's general education requirements continue to be debated. Amidst considerable controversy and national attention, Stanford faculty recently approved changes to the core that will expand its international and multicultural dimensions. Never in question, however, has been the importance of a core for all students —including engineers—that provides a broad introduction to their cultural and intellectual heritage.

For more information, contact Thomas Wasow, Dean of Undergraduate Studies, Building 1, Stanford University, Stanford, Calif. 94305.

CHAPTER FOUR

CRITERIA AND STRATEGIES

ESSENTIAL UNDERGRADUATE EXPERIENCES

KEY CRITERIA FOR COURSEWORK

ADMINISTRATIVE STRATEGIES

IMPROVING H&SS ACADEMIC ADVISING

FINDING PRINCIPLES OF COHERENCE

SOME SAMPLE COURSE CLUSTERS

INTEGRATING LEARNING

Every effort to improve H&SS coursework has to work within a particular setting. Many of the programs described in the previous chapter have developed in settings unusually supportive of the liberal arts. Many have benefited by special funding, top administrative leadership, entrepreneurship on the part of committed faculty, and other advantages that programs cannot always count on. The question arises, then, of whether progress is possible in more typical settings and, if so, through what steps it can be achieved.

A "typical" setting in this context is an engineering school in a medium-to-large university. Its students seek professional training; liberal education tends to rank low among their goals. Between research, teaching, maintaining laboratories, consulting, meeting professional responsibilities, and perhaps supervising graduate students, faculty also feel they have priorities other than the liberal education of undergraduates. The institution is among that 90 percent that, according to AAC data, offer no interdisciplinary courses integrating the perspectives and subject matters of liberal arts and engineering. Students fulfill their H&SS requirements by choosing among conventional free-standing arts and sciences courses. By tradition and preference, liberal education is left to liberal arts faculty who, at this typical institution, are themselves inattentive to the needs of engineers. Since advising is weak, students are, as one engineering educator has put it, "in effect pushed out the door, told to go across the street to the college of arts and sciences, and to choose any five or six courses there that can satisfy ABET." This the students do, with results we have seen documented in Chapter Two.

There are steps that can be taken in such environments to improve H&SS coursework, even within ABET's minimal requirements. "Typical" engineering schools are resistant but not impervious to H&SS reform. Those seeking to improve H&SS coursework in these settings, however, may need to give special thought to their goals, resources, and strategies. They may need to consider what should be sought from liberal study as well as the criteria that should govern liberal study. They should have a clear sense of the kinds of courses and course combinations through which students can best pursue liberal education at their institutions. They will want, finally, to find the most effective ways of creating systems and a climate that will support the new emphasis.

The remaining pages review these key considerations and suggest particular organizational and educational strategies. They spell out sound criteria for H&SS coursework, and identify joint efforts to improve academic advising as the key to H&SS reform. They advocate a strategy of helping students discover appropriate and personally meaningful principles of coherence for their H&SS coursework. They suggest as examples, finally, a number of themes appealing to different needs and interests, and illustrate how arts and sciences courses available at most institutions can be affectively combined to explore them.

ESSENTIAL UNDERGRADUATE EXPERIENCES

A sound starting point for thinking about the proper goals of the H&SS component is *Integrity in the College Curriculum: A Report to the Academic Community*, published in 1985 by the Association of American Colleges. "Integrity," as it has come to be known, identifies nine "experiences," "skills," or "ways of understanding" as essential to any undergraduate education. We list them below, with a few lines

on each also drawn from the report.
- *Inquiry, abstract logical thinking, critical analysis.* To reason well, to recognize when reason and evidence are not enough, to discover the legitimacy of intuition, to subject inert data to the probing analysis of the mind—these are the primary experiences required of the undergraduate course of study.
- *Literacy: writing, reading, speaking, listening.* A bachelor's degree should mean that its holders can read, write, and speak at levels of distinction and have been given many opportunities to learn how. It should also mean that many do so with style.
- *Understanding numerical data.* Students should encounter concepts that permit a sophisticated response to arguments and positions which depend on numbers and statistics. Such concepts would include degree of risk, scatter, uncertainty, orders of magnitude, rates of change, confidence levels and acceptability, and the interpretation of graphs as they are manifest in numbers.
- *Historical consciousness.* The more refined our historical understanding, the better prepared we are to recognize complexity, ambiguity, and uncertainty as intractable conditions of human society.
- *Science.* [Students should not only understand the scientific method, but also study the] human, social, and political implications of scientific research.
- *Values.* [M]en and women ... must make real choices, assume responsibility for their decisions, be comfortable with their own behavior, and know why. They must embody the values of a democratic society in order to fulfill the responsibilities of citizenship. They must be equipped to be perceptive and wise critics of that society, repositories of the values that make civilized and humane society possible.
- *Art.* Without a knowledge of the language of the fine arts, we see less and hear less. Without some experience in the performing arts we are denied the knowledge of disciplined creativity.
- *International and multicultural experiences.* Colleges must create a curriculum in which the insights and understandings, the lives and aspirations of the distant and foreign, the different and neglected, are more widely comprehended by their graduates.
- *Study in depth.* Depth requires sequential learning, building on blocks of knowledge that lead to more sophisticated understanding and encourage leaps of imagination and efforts at synthesis.

Engineering students have several of these essential experiences as they complete their standard programs in mathematics, natural sciences, and engineering science. Yet for literacy, historical consciousness, investigation

> A coherent program of study is one in which the diverse intellectual experiences provided by students' different courses are somehow integrated into a larger structure of understanding

of values, encounters with the arts, international and multicultural exposures, and even for experience with many modes of inquiry and analysis, they must look largely to their H&SS components. These few liberal arts courses, in short, in large part represent the engineer's opportunity to acquire the knowledge, skills, and habits of thought necessary to learning throughout life. They largely define, that is, the opportunity for general education. As a result, the primary expectation of any H&SS component should be that it serve that end.

The more a set of H&SS courses meets other key criteria, the more likely it is to provide a general education. These include adequate size, breadth, depth, and coherence of study, and the capacity to engage the individual. We consider these criteria now in turn.

KEY CRITERIA FOR COURSEWORK

The consensus of those who have looked carefully at the ABET minimum standards for H&SS coursework seems to be that they are too low. The undergraduate engineering curriculum, averaging 134 semester hours in length, is already overburdened with subject matter requirements. Nonetheless, it is probably untenable to expect meaningful results within an H&SS component of only sixteen semester hours—a little over five courses or 12.5 percent for student's total coursework. Some observers endorse the recommendation first made in 1944 by the Society for the Promotion of Engineering Education (now the American Society for Engineering Education) that at least 20 percent of all coursework be in H&SS and writing—a standard that would ensure at least seven to eight courses within H&SS per se.[27] In any case, engineering schools should themselves consider requiring more of their students. An effective strategy for many would be to reclaim as H&SS electives one or more courses now designated as free electives. Some might consider as well requiring one less engineering course. In every such case, however, considerations of marginal value should point to the wisdom of the change. As George Bugliarello, president of New York's Polytechnic University, has put it, past a certain point of technical competence it is better that engineers "be able to ask ... important questions that affect our survival as a society than learn one more higher-order differential equation."[28]

Breadth and depth are relative terms, but at least a measure of each seems essential to a well-constructed H&SS component. Breadth, in the form of study within separate and diverse liberal arts disciplines, assures experience with some of the different modes of knowing that characterize work in the humanities and social sciences. Depth, consisting in some degree of concentration and usually of advanced coursework in a discipline or subject area, conveys both the possibilities and limits of such study. By giving the student a sense of how actually to acquire and use knowledge in a given field, it provides a foundation for self-directed and lifelong learning that may be particularly important to the engineer.

The degrees of breadth and depth that are possible will vary with the size of the H&SS component. Students might reasonably be expected, however, to take at least one course each in the humanities, the social sciences and the arts, and in either of the first two of these areas a course in two or more separate disciplines. In the terms employed in Chapter Two, this pattern would provide minimum breadth across H&SS areas and breadth within one of them. At the same time some advanced coursework should be required to ensure at least minimal depth.

Both breadth and depth of coursework typically contribute to coherence. The latter, however, is far more important in and of itself as a criterion of H&SS coursework. A coherent program of study is one in which the diverse intellectual experiences provided by students' different courses are somehow integrated into a larger structure of understanding. Achieving coherence therefore requires a selection of courses that at least implicitly connect in some meaningful way with one another—often as examinations from different vantage points of some common set of themes and issues. It also requires the student's active reflection on and synthesis of his or her learning. When these two conditions are met, a course of study becomes more than the sum of its parts—an important fact to engineering students who have so few H&SS courses with which to work.

A final important criterion of H&SS coursework is its capacity to engage the engineering student. An MIT undergraduate recently quoted in the national press may or may not have exaggerated when she said that most engineeers regard liberal arts courses as "unnecessary evils."[29] Clearly, however, ways should be found for engineers to obtain a general education while at the same time pursuing meaningful individual interests and concerns. If engineering students can identify worthy areas of interest that lend themselves to exploration across humanities and social sciences disciplines, these may provide them the best possible principles for organizing their H&SS courses. Individual passions, concerns, interests, and curiosities can structure, motivate, and animate selection of H&SS courses. They can bring meaning and enjoyment to what can otherwise be a series of isolated activities and exposures to inert ideas, and they can seduce students into a lifelong habit of taking responsibility for their own learning.

These, then, are key criteria for the H&SS component: an emphasis on general education, adequate size, breadth, depth, coherence, and the capacity to engage the individual student. Coursework meeting these standards would go far toward answering the frequent calls from the engineering profession for more efficient and "more carefully structured" H&SS components.[30] It would win new respect for, and attention to, H&SS coursework from liberal arts faculty. It would be consistent with the intentions behind ABET's prescriptions—including (for reasons spelled out in Chapter One) the requirement that liberal arts coursework reflect an appropriate professional rationale. Most importantly, it would represent an important advance over typical student practice, achieved without sacrifice of students' freedom of choice. The question remains, however, of how coursework of such quality can be achieved in what we have defined as typical settings and how these criteria might translate into particular course selections by real students.

ADMINISTRATIVE STRATEGIES

Modest, practical steps can often begin to create a climate and provide support for better H&SS coursework. What can be accomplished in a given setting will, of course, depend on myriad factors, and appropriate strategies will vary. But given an open-minded administration and an engineering faculty that is no worse than generally disinterested, advocates might begin by working for the appointment of an ad hoc committee to be charged with several tasks. The first of these would be to examine H&SS coursework policy and practice locally—that is, to look at catalogues, transcripts, and other materials in order to document the actual nature and extent of any shortcomings. The second charge would be to open a dialogue between faculty in engineering and their liberal arts colleagues concerning appropriate educational objectives for H&SS coursework and ways of achieving these objectives on the particular campus. The work of such a committee can provide the basis for a factual, broad-based report that can raise awareness of any problem and create support and concrete proposals for change.

Many engineering schools will see some wisdom in assigning coordinating responsibility for the improvement of H&SS coursework to an appropriate administrator—perhaps an assistant dean—supported by an active advisory group that includes faculty and administrators from both engineering and the liberal arts. If and when proposals for changes in program policy are adopted, this kind of broadly representative group can help develop the printed materials that will be needed by faculty, advisors, and students if they are to understand the changes and respond productively to the intentions behind them. It can oversee the continuing process of orientation, monitoring, and evaluation that is needed to insure that policy is followed and, where necessary, appropriately modified. It can assist with such seemingly mundane but critical tasks as seeing that important humanities and social sciences courses are available to engineers at hours when they can take them.

IMPROVING H&SS ACADEMIC ADVISING

Whatever strategies are followed and whatever administrative structures and processes are established, in most institutions academic advising will provide the best point of intervention. Academic advising is scandalously poor in higher education. The H&SS advising of engineering students is worse than most. ABET charges faculty with seeing that it is done well and, according to AAC's survey, in some 73 percent of programs engineering faculty themselves carry the responsibility. One need not cite extreme examples of ratios of five hundred students to one H&SS advisor to make the point that faculty do not always take the obligation seriously. The results reported in Chapter Two speak for themselves. In most settings, the improvement of advising would provide enormous leverage. The advising conference is, or can be made, a required stop for every student prior to each term's registration. It exerts, or can be made to exert, great influence over H&SS course selection. If nothing else is done to improve liberal studies, faculty and/or professional advisors should at least work regularly with students to help them plan and follow a course of study meeting the criteria set forth in the preceeding pages.

Academic advising is a high calling, but one many engineering faculty will be reluctant to commit more time to, especially if doing so means counseling students in the liberal arts. Their reluctance is understandable. They have a right to expect help from their institutions in getting this job done. The provision of general education is an institutional responsibility vested largely with the arts and sciences faculty members. Whenever necessary, institutions should release a portion of the latter's time (or that of professional advisors knowledgeable about general education) to help advise on H&SS coursework. There are colleges and universities at which engineering faculty do all H&SS advising. There are others where liberal arts faculty take responsibility for this task. Still others draw on advisors from both engineering and the liberal arts (in part, on one campus, through regular group advising sessions that bring together members of each faculty). The point, however, is not so much how it is done. The point is that it be done, by advisors who take their task seriously and have the knowledge and resources to help students make wise choices.

What counsel will good advisors give their engineering students? Since at typical institutions the H&SS component has to be put together from currently offered arts and sciences courses, engineering students need first to be alert to many of the same considerations in choosing courses as their peers in the arts and sciences. They should realize, for example, that courses in such fields as economics and organizational psychology—when taught within the arts and sciences—will often be less "applied" in approach and have more value as general education than comparable offerings within a business school. They should know, however, that the content and approach of a specific course and the quality of its instructor should always weigh more heavily in their judgment of its value than its departmental home, title, or apparent fit within some sequence of study. Engineers should be encouraged to find alternatives to large lecture-style courses, especially when these are customarily staffed by teaching assistants, and they should avoid courses that are textbook-driven. Advisors should help them seek out classes with smaller enrollments and courses that emphasize writing and discussion. And so that they can learn not just "about" a few arts and sciences disciplines but also something of how one actually "does" them, engineers, like all students, should also be pointed toward courses requiring the analysis of primary texts, original artifacts, and primary data.

FINDING PRINCIPLES OF COHERENCE

In working to discover principles of coherence for the H&SS component, advisors may need to be more conscious of their advisees as engineers. The ideal, again, is to find substantive areas of inquiry that are compelling to the individual student and that lend themselves to exploration across humanities and social science disciplines. Many engineering students readily identify appropriate H&SS coursework connecting in some direct way with their major. Providing other criteria are met, the industrial engineering major can construct an entirely appropriate H&SS component focusing, for example, on psychology; the civil engineering major a component on the social environment; and the electrical engineering major a component on language development. Other engineering students construct with equal ease H&SS components that have no explicit connection to their major field or to interests traditionally associated with the engineer. They engage comfortably with the humanities, arts, and social sciences—entirely on those disciplines' own terms. Far more often, however, helping the engineeering student achieve intellectual investment in H&SS coursework is a task that requires some work.

Few first-year students arrive on campus with well developed appropriate interests, and most should be strongly encouraged to use their earliest H&SS coursework for exploration. Before they are far into their programs they should begin reflecting, with their advisors' help, on which of their developing interests and needs suggest promising directions for H&SS study. There is no point, however, at which the shaping of a direction needs to be complete. The continuing testing and redefining of a coherent course of liberal study and the grounds of one's engagement with it can itself be a valuable educational process. Drawing on all the student is learning and thinking about, it can and should extend over a student's entire undergraduate experience—and beyond.

There are innumerable themes, subjects, issues, and questions that might provide appropriate coherence to an engineer's undergraduate course of H&SS study. We are indebted to Lance Schachterle, a project consultant from Wooster Polytechnic Institute, for the following suggestions:

☐ *Technology studies.* Many students might be interested in a course of studies that sharpens their ability to discern technology's intended and unintended consequences for society. Students pursuing this theme might combine a course in the history of science and technology with numerous relevant offerings in other areas of the humanities, social sciences, and the arts. Among their other concerns, all of these courses would in some way shed light on the ways in which "progress" and modern technology shape the lives we lead.

☐ *Philosophical issues in technology.* Students whose interests in the effects of technology are more conceptual than instrumental (as in the previous option) might enjoy a set of courses considering, among other things, broad questions of values and ethics that arise from modern technology. Drawing on numerous disciplines they might, for example, examine the relationship between technology and science; explore what, if any, human forces are directing the growth of contemporary technology; and debate (as do Ellul, Heidegger, and Florman) in what sense, if any, technology makes people "free." This option could also provide opportunities for searching explorations of professional ethics.

☐ *Cognitive sciences.* From Leonardo's model of the human eye as a "camera obscura" to today's computers, we have used ideas or images from technology to think about how we think. Modern technology, most notably in the computer fields, has contributed substantially to the debates over human cognition, and many students (especially in computer science and electrical engineering/communications) would be interested in courses dealing with the themes of the cognitive sciences. Philosophy, epistemology, psychology, and anthropology and linguisitics could offer support to such a theme. Students might explore, for example, the contemporary "mind/ brain" debate—whether cognition can be explained mechanistically by accounting for thinking as definable physical processes in the brain. The computer as a model for the brain, with the related issues of defining thinking, originality, and "artificial intelligence," would figure heavily in such a sequence.

☐ *Aesthetics and design.* Aesthetic factors can figure importantly in engineering design. Interdisciplinary studies in the humanities (especially history), the social sciences (pyschology of perception), and the arts can build on and advance students' interest and understanding in this dimension of professional activity. Students should pursue, where available, coursework that considers distinctive aesthetic and technological achievements within a cultural framework (as, for example, the art of Greece, the Orient, the Middle Ages, Weimar Germany, and the like).

☐ *The arts.* Engineering faculty often report that their students have strong interests in the visual and performing arts (especially music). Courses of possible interest might include work in literature, pyschology, folklore, anthropology, and history, as well as offerings in the arts themselves. The reliance of many contemporary forms of the arts on modern technology (electronics in music and theater, holography and lasers in the visual arts) also makes possible many intersections between engineering and areas of the arts students may wish to pursue.

☐ *Science, technology, and literature.* Stretching from the works of Bacon and Swift to those of contemporary writers, there is a rich tradition of imaginative literature that, among other concerns, speculates broadly on the consequences and directions of science and technology and their meaning for humankind. Many courses in history, philosophy, and sociology can be appropriate complements to the literature courses that would consider the imaginative constructions and themes of this tradition.

□ *Public policy.* Technology raises many questions about legal systems and policy decisions. For example, new medical technologies require the definition or redefinition of human life from conception through death. Sophisticated technologies (for example, computers and interactive fiber-communications networks) raise the specter of "Big Brother," and require rethinking of laws of privacy. Lay people in court cases must often sort out conflicting evidence from experts on the affects of new technology. Scientists and engineers figure prominently in the debates over the feasibility and policy implications of the Strategic Defense Initiative. A combination of social science courses stressing social organizations and legal systems, with philosophy, history, or literature courses, could ground students in a variety of the issues technology raises for public-policy makers.

□ *Management.* The perspectives of the humanities and social sciences have much to offer engineering students interested in management. Not only economics, but history, sociology, pyschology, and literature are rich sources of insight into the manager's task and environment. These insights are applicable, of course, to the management of people, but they are of central importance to functions such as investment and marketing as well.

□ *Environment, energy, and resources.* Many economics, history, political science, philosophy, and literature departments offer courses of potential interest to students with environmental concerns. Coverage in appropriate courses might include such issues as the use and management of the American wilderness; social, legal, and health consequences of resource development and energy generation; the ethics and economics of resource recovery; and attitudes toward land usage.

□ *International studies.* As technology, especially communications, makes international access easier, engineering students will find mastering the language and history of other cultures increasingly valuable. Multinational corporate structures and international markets require familiarity with cultures other than one's own. Concerns about technology transfer and foreign competition are widespread. Since ABET now permits beginning-level language courses to count as H&SS, programs could include study of a foreign language beginning at any level.

□ *American studies.* An important variant of international studies is the study by international students of American language, history, and culture. Usually sponsors of these international students expect that they will acquire skills in English and become familiar with American culture, especially in management, during their undergraduate studies.

The topics listed are illustrative only. One can easily imagine other good themes—The Great Ideas, for example, or The Nature of Work and Profession. Again, there is much to be learned in the process of discovering one's own interests and concerns and in developing a coherent program of H&SS study to explore them.

SOME SAMPLE COURSE CLUSTERS

Let us now illustrate how arts and sciences courses available at most institutions might be combined under several such headings to fulfill appropriate criteria for H&SS study. The suggestions that follow were among several sample clusters devised by participants in the working conference of engineering educators—most of them deans or faculty members in engineering or the liberal arts—convened by AAC at the Belmont Conference Center in Maryland in October 1987. More of their suggestions will appear in a later AAC publication for H&SS advisors and students.

An engineering student with an interest in technology studies might begin with four basic courses: "Introduction to Philosophy"; "History of Western (or World) Civilization"; "Introduction to Social Psychology"; and "American (or English) Literature of the Nineteenth (or Twentieth) Century." Provided, as always, that they were well taught, these four courses would provide valuable general education, breadth across the areas of the humanities and social sciences, and breadth within the humanities as well. They would help develop the student's interests and frame of reference and give him or her the foundation for planning more advanced H&SS study. For some students, this might take the form of enrollment in two intermediate-level courses like the history of science and technology and the history of the Industrial Revolution (including the period after World War II). These courses would build on the earlier history of Western (or World) civilization course and provide considerable depth. A seventh optional course in either cultural anthropology or public-policy study could provide additional breadth at an advanced level, and help round out the student's understanding of the issue as it affects and is affected by other areas of concern. The particular courses in such a cluster would all be chosen for a reason—for example, the nineteenth century literature course because it would probably reflect the rise of modern, Western, industrialized culture; the philosophy course because it would give training in critical thinking and a context in which to understand arguments of value; and the cultural anthropology course because of its multicultural perspective. Equally valid technology studies clusters could be assembled from other courses. The important thing would be for the student to make a thoughtful selection consistent with the sound criteria.

Students with an interest in the international studies area will usually have a particular country or region in mind as a focus of study. Developing relevant language competency at a level compatible with at least two years of college study should be a first concern. Students with a strong background of study in high school may be able to achieve this competency in fewer than two years of study and then have the time, if they wish, to acquire more advanced language skills. Another important foundation might be a course in the history of the area of interest—for example, for the student studying French, a course in the history and culture of France, or indeed of Francophone Africa. A basic course in the social sciences might be cultural anthropology. In some settings, offerings might be available that focus on the region of interest, but a more broad-based cultural anthropology course—presenting the methods, concerns, and general message of the discipline—would also be valuable. A number of courses suggest themselves as internationally oriented electives. Within the humanities, students might consider a foreign-language literature course, preferably in the language in question, but perhaps in translation in cases when that is not feasible. Other humanities options could include courses in the region's dominant religious traditions (for example, Islam and Judaism in the Middle East) and in the history of its art. Within the social sciences, students might consider coursework in international economic development (focusing in part on the spread of technology to the developing world) and in comparative politics or sociology. Clusters coherently assembled along these lines would be likely to provide interested students considerable general education and breadth. They also would encourage a deepening comprehension of not only other languages and language communities but ultimately of other cultures and civilizations.

A third paradigm illustrates what H&SS advisors can do for those students who, at least at the outset of their college careers, genuinely do not know what their interests might be. Because these students, more than others, may need to explore broadly, they might simply be encouraged to begin with a basic course—perhaps even a good survey—in each of the three areas of the arts, the humanities, and the social sciences, and thereafter to build a sequence or two with courses at the intermediate, or intermediate and advanced, levels. The starting point might be courses in history, economics, and music for one student, and philosophy, art, and political science for another. The principal sequences for two such engineers might develop in economics and political science, respectively. Although some taking this path might never identify interests broad and strong enough to support a coherent H&SS component, they would not forfeit depth, breadth, and general education either. As one arts and sciences dean has remarked, "they wouldn't do themselves any harm."

A final example, appropriate for students with or without focused interests, is an H&SS component built around the Great Ideas. Coursework might begin, for example, with study of the Old Testament or of Greek literature and thought in translation. It might include courses (variations of which are offered in the humanities, arts, or social sciences) examining classical works and seminal ideas in such key periods in the development of Western thought as the Renaissance (including Shakespeare), the Enlightenment (Voltaire and Adam Smith), and the late eighteenth and nineteenth centuries (classicism and romanticism). Subsequent courses could address the end of synthesis and the beginning of the modern and postmodern breakdown. One, for example, might be an offering in modern art, the feminist revolution, or alternative futures; another might be a seminar on a focal figure like Freud, Marx, or Darwin. This kind of cluster, too, presents opportunities for breadth, depth, and general education. It represents the classic answer of the liberal arts to the question, "What ought every educated person know?"

INTEGRATING LEARNING

Each of these four sample H&SS components—and all others like them—are far more likely to be coherent if the responsibility for making them so does not rest entirely with the student. Ideally, students should have frequent and substantial opportunities to reflect on and integrate what they have learned, and they should have the guidance of faculty in doing so. As a first step, liberal arts faculty need to concern themselves with the interconnections among their courses; they need to work with their colleagues to ensure complementarity in what they offer. They will then be better able, and more inclined, to help students taking given course combinations discover at every step what their work is adding up to. So-called "capstone" experiences can be especially helpful. They may be offered as a senior seminar within a humanities or social sciences department or offered to engineers as a culminating interdisciplinary design project. Students may need to arrange their own capstone experiences, perhaps as tutorials

CRITERIA AND STRATEGIES

or independent-study projects under the direction of professors. In any case, all engineers need such opportunities to draw together their work in the humanities and social sciences, and it is critical that they be encouraged and helped to find these opportunities.

The contents of this volume—empirical findings, program descriptions, and recommendations—all converge on a few simple points. Engineering education is an unfinished design, and many hands must have a part in completing it. There are major roles for ABET, for institutional and program administrators, and for engineering and liberal arts faculty. In indicating some of the steps that can be taken, we have focused on the importance of well-conceived course selection and emphasized the centrality of sound criteria and good advising. The current state of H&SS coursework, however, is such that almost any form of attention can be beneficial. Some will see in this fact an indictment of engineering education. We see in it a critical need, and an important and exciting opportunity.

REFERENCES

1. Samuel C. Florman, *The Civilized Engineer* (New York: St. Martin's Press, 1987), 169-170.
2. Edmund T. Cranch and George M. Nordby, "Engineering Education: At the Crossroads Without a Compass?" *Engineering Education* 76 (May 1986): 73.
3. William K. LeBold, "Humanities and Social Science in Engineering: A Survey of Research Perspectives" (commissioned background paper, Purdue University, 1986), 16-21.
4. Cranch and Nordby, "Engineering Education," 743.
5. "Survey Results," *Spectrum* 21 (June 1984): 59-63. See also "Job Satisfaction Rises with Age, Survey Reports," *The Institute* 9 (November 1985): 1; and Florman, *The Civilized Engineer*, 176.
6. "Trends in Engineering Degree Awards: 1972-1984," *U.S. Department of Education Office of Educational Research and Improvement Bulletin*, (January 1987): 2.
7. LeBold, "Humanities and Social Science in Engineering," 10-11.
8. National Research Council Committee on the Education and Utilization of the Engineer, *Engineering Education and Practice in the United States: Foundations of Our Techno-Economic Future* (Washington, D.C.: National Academy Press, 1958), 73.
9. Rank orderings by Clifford Adelman, "To Compete or Not Compete," forthcoming in *Educational Record* 69 (Spring 1988), based on data in Jerilee Grandy, *Ten Year Trends in SAT Scores and Other Characteristics of High School Seniors Taking the SAT and Planning to Study Mathematics, Science and Engineering*, Research Report RR-87-49 (Princeton: Educational Testing Service, 1987). The cohorts are: mathematics and statistics, computer sciences, physical science, architecture and environmental engineering, life sciences, earth and environmental science, pyschology, social science, interdisciplinary and other sciences, engineering, pre-medical, other health fields, pre-law, humanities, history and culture, foreign languages, studio and performing arts, communications, business, education, vocational fields, and all others.
10. National Research Council, *Engineering Education and Practice in the United States*, 74.
11. "Report of the Working Group on the Humanities and Social Sciences Curriculum" (Massachusetts Institute of Technology, April 30, 1985), 9.
12. Samuel C. Florman, "Toward Liberal Learning for Engineers," *Technology Review* 89 (February/March 1986): 18.
13. *Criteria for Accrediting Programs in Engineering in the United States: Effective for Evaluations During 1986-1987 Academic Year* (New York: Accreditation Board for Engineering and Technology, 1986), 7.
14. Florman, "Toward Liberal Learn-

ing for Engineers," 23.
15. "Report of the Working Group," 8.
16. Florman, The Civilized Engineer, 183.
17. "Curricular Content of Bachelor's Degrees," U.S. Department of Education Office of Education Research and Improvement Bulletin (November 1986): 6.
18. "Report of the Working Group," 10, 35.
19. Cranch and Nordby, "Engineering Education," 746.
20. Criteria for Accrediting Programs, 6.
21. F. D. Schaumburg, "Engineering—As If People Mattered," Civil Engineering (October 1981): 50-58. See also I. C. Goulter, "How Effective is the Humanities and Social Science Component?" Engineering Education 75 (January 1985): 215-217.
22. Criteria for Accrediting Programs, 7.
23. "Toward Richer Experiences in Humanities and Social Sciences," Technology Review 90 (August/September 1987): 3.
24. "MIT Faculty Call for 'Recasting' of Undergraduate Curriculum," Engineering Education News 13 (January 1987): 5.
25. Florman, The Civilized Engineer, 3-4.
26. Ibid., 3-4.
27. Florman, The Civilized Engineer, 199.
28. George Bugliarello as quoted in Judith Axler Turner, "Professors Find Many Obstacles to Combining Technology and Liberal Arts in Single Course," Chronicle of Higher Education, 4 March 1987, 14-15.
29. Isbell Brecht as quoted in Edward B. Fiske, "MIT Widens Engineering Training," New York Times, 1 June 1987, 12.
30. "Reassessment of Engineering and Engineering Technology Studies," Engineering Education 67 (May 1977): recommendation 3. See also Goulter, "How Effective is the Humanities and Social Science Component?" 217.